Connecting

GERALD MIDDENTS

CONNECTING

iUniverse books may be ordered through booksellers or by contacting:

iUniverse
1663 Liberty Drive
Bloomington, IN 47403
www.iuniverse.com
844-349-9409

ISBN: 978-1-6632-3973-0 (sc)
ISBN: 978-1-6632-3972-3 (e)

Print information available on the last page.

iUniverse rev. date: 05/09/2022

CONTENTS

MEANING DIMENSIONS

Humans explore depths and heights!
  Countering shallow surface insights!
    People become intrigues by meaning!
    As we search for reasons to be living!
  This requires internalized reflections
Bounced against our future directions!

Looking both backward & forward
  Clarifies where to move onward!
    Life may continue to be in a flow!
    Discovering more mysteries to know!
  The past provides us known platforms
For launching ahead into the storms!

Rough waves call for anchorage!
  Holding us fast in times of alarms!
    Threats test our own limitations
    To balance realities & aspirations!
  Faith, Families, Friends in situations
Strengthen capacities for innovations!

HOW MEANING EMERGES

Meaning is an intangible quality!
  Needing secure anchors in reality!
    Meaning does not ride on the surface!
    Rather, it emerges out of our purpose!

What are the challenges in our days?
Confronting humans to seek new ways!

In dark deep, we hope for light!
To brighten our way to heights!
Very important are key questions!
Helping us to find new directions!
Meaning arises from foundations
Lifting us upward toward heavens!

This search brings out of shadows!
Attracting us to rise from darkness!
Life becomes illuminated in lights!
Helping us to discover new insights!
Building on firm stones of wisdom
Meaning inspires our ne rhythms!

WIDER MEANING

Surfacing brings us into the light!
Interacting with ones who are bright!
Exchanging perspectives can be helpful!
Broadening our horizons is delightful!
We discover new findings with insight
Our meaning may reach new heights!

The wider foundations are desirable!
Appreciating how to be more capable!
Broader landscapes help our visions!

Making us more confident in decisions!
We widen our base as inter-disciplinary!
Overcoming narrow fields with variety!

Breadth helps us see more possibilities!
Bolstering our strengths in creativities!
Width fosters meaning to be inclusive
Overcoming propensity to be exclusive!
Our broader world is commendable
Including views so we are bendable!

HIGHER MEANING!

Ascending to heights is breadth-taking!
Air is thin; Scope enlargement exciting!
Horizons are infinite; Uplifting our vision!
Our human limits narrow appreciations!
Meaning expands about all creation!
Prompting us to make new inventions!

Our depth and breadth are essential!
In order that we aspire to potentials!
Personal meaning becomes intangible!
Perceived inwardly & always malleable!
Thin oxygen could make us pliable
Vulnerable to mindsets suggestible!

Stretching us to reach new heights!
Contributing to expand our insights
Our live are then further transformed!
As creative creatures, meaning emerges!
Humanity benefits by new experiences
Inspiring all to try new experiments!

SPIRALING

As depth, widths, heights combine!
Into spiraling dimensions refined!
Imagine rotations that can take off!
So that additional spins take us aloft!
Exciting sensations inspire more
Finding new avenues to explore!

Consider images of RNA and DNA!
Carrying genes for new generations!
Their future will involve exploration!
So expansive meaning finds its ways!
The foundations we have built upon
Hopefully will carry their creations!

Spirals engage future humanity
To explore life more meaningfully!
Passing forward our experiences
Provides posterity with dimensions!
Our insights in meaning may expand!
Enlarging hopeful vision for them!

Preface

Since we were conceived, us have had many connections. Initially, we were connected to our Mothers. In many families, we Would have sisters or brothers. Our Father had numerous ways of Connecting with us.

Playmates became our broader interactions as friendships Developed. In school, classmates were our co-learners. Teammates Were vital to engage in activities and in sports. Social occasions expanded informal meetings along with choirs, dramas and dates.

Young adult collaborations grow into traveling and career explorations. Co-workers and customers stretched our professional Development. We learned civil rather than criminal activities. Responsible citizenship involved us in collegiality, religions, voting and military service.

Yes, connections expand socially and professionally, We May marry a mate and become parents. Maturing as a person Becomes an enlarging network.

The following poetry is designed to value and appreciate our collaborations.

I. AWESOME FUTURE

A. LET's CONNECT:

Humans can facilitate <u>connecting!</u>
Relating usually happens locally!
Increasingly we can connect globally!
The global internet helps by facilitating!

Exchanging messages is very essential!
This helps humanity reach our potential!
Communicating is our specialized prize
Interacting helps humanity become wise!

Relationships expect us to be <u>listening!</u>
Moreover, this may reduce arguing!
These connections are worthwhile!
So that exchanging is our style!

How could we exist without relating?
Others as partners are typically waiting!
Partnerships require communicating
This enriches our life for our living!

These interactions involve <u>creating!</u>
Partners expect to be interacting!
A negative comes when destroying!
This really undoes further building!

Humans are ingenuous in creativity!
This is contagious to be done globally!
There are major problems to solve!
Expecting all of us to become involved!

Another key in relating is <u>supporting!</u>
This key counters negative rejecting!
Humans are actually social creatures!
Socializing is a significant feature!

Other creatures teach us a great deal!
Their socializing shows up very real!
Supporting builds up new experiences!
From God, families, mates and communities!

Collaborating is a very profound process;
God takes initiative to establish our faith!
He becomes the foundation of connecting
We are in fellowship for then relating.

Communities of faith have their mission,
So, relating persons to is our commission.
We have connections with friends and family,
Thereby, we hopefully become our ministry.

This creates our connectional Church;
We then engage jointly in worship.
We reach outward and inward;
Sharing together God's Word.

<u>ZOOM</u> expands over the globe;
Users can examine and probe.
This outreach enlarge outreach;
As participants from land and beach.

Has Science replaced Angelology?
People always try to explain mystery.
For centuries, humans used angelology;
But not very often in the last century.

Scientific hypotheses are provocative;
Researchers try to find locate as objective.
Scientific methods search for more evidence;
That satisfies the researchers and Scientists.

UNIFYING CONNECTIONS vs.
VIOLENT SEPARATIONS

WIDER COLLABORATING

Here are recollections of collaborating;
Including Sabbaticals for learning.
Professors benefit from experience;
Crucial updating came each time.

A Seminar at the Jung Institute in
"Psychology and Religion" in focus.
A semester in Washington, D.C.
Center for Theology and Public Policy.

In 1984, A conference in Russia;
I spoke about enemy-making.[1]
"Why Do We Make Enemies"
With difficulties "Letting Them Go?"

My brief comments in the Kremlin.
My photo shown in MOSCOW NEWS!
Re-invited to USSR in 1986 and 1988
Family illness prevented these trips.

---

[1] Middents, G., 2007, <u>BRIDGING FEAR and PEACE: From Bullying to Doing Justice,</u> Manipal University Press.

3

U.S.<> USSR. Pursued peace-making!
The "Cold War" then was resulting.
Both have huge nuclear weapons.
Non-Violence for decades keeps on.

My reflections are very positive!
Domestically and also internationally.
Opportunities opened locally and globally;
My own efforts have been met very readily!

These connections were very special!
By helping to relate international!
This was also very meaningful;
For further times a wonderful.

Rotary International has a project;
To eradicate polio globally and quick.
In 2004, Carol and I joined another team;
We inoculated Indian children under five!!

Then onward to Asia in Viet Nam;
Hosted by "Binh" and "Mr. No Problem!"
They both connected with us very well;
They are very likeable and memorable!

International friends are special;
I recall that they are essential!
They spoke very clearly in English
Making me feel distinguished!

Thomas John invited me to India;
He hosted me in the state of Kerala.
His Faculty wanted help in Psychology
At a college in Mahatma Gandhi University.

Thomas is also a Christian Minister;
He opened invitations to be speaker

At his own Union Christian College
Plus, churches and to Rotarians.

I worked through his connections;
For a Master's Degree in Psychology;
Plus, groups in this community.
We established more exchanges.

Later, UCC could award a Ph.D.
This attracted even more students.
Thomas and I had collegiality
Our joint efforts had vitality1

Alan Geyer and I met in Washington, DC
At the Center for Theology and Public Policy.
Alan was Director as an interdisciplinarian
He had networks that explored broadly.

Alan helped me to connect with Russia
We both joined a delegation in 1984.
Hosted by the Russian Orthodox Church
And the National Council of Churches.

My brief remarks in the Kremlin were
On both Enemy-making and Peace-Making.
This got attention in the MOSCOW NEWS,
Representing an exchange of views.

Later delegation in 1986 and 1988
But then my wife became very ill.
I had to cancel these two trips,
As she died in May of 1988.

Churches and organizations in Texas
Invited me to provide local lectures.
The "Cold War" then later ended
As these two world powers related.

Human dynamics are powerful and vulnerable!
A force one-way will prompt a counter force!
Firing a gun requires the holder to react!
Punching a computer with a spring back!

Launching a rocket forces a big blast!
Gravity holds jumpers return to earth!
Now global warming produces a reaction!
Connecting nations incites political action!

Regional tensions can lead to violence!
Conflicts result that lack tolerance!
People readily separate for calm!
Humans search for easy balm!

Interference may meet resentment!
Many will protect their investments!
No wonder there are conflicts globally
Disputes are often not settled readily!

FOCUS

This poem addresses difficult issues!
Groups separating are torn like tissue!
Leaving tears and "taxes" as painful!
Plus, uncertainties as unpredictable!

The scale of movement is big and small!
Tribal-like families to huge cultures!
Global conditions are gradually evolving!
Many problems are in need of soon solving!

HUMAN BRAINS CONNECT

Human beings have amazing brains!
Estimates of over 83 billion neurons!
Twelve times people on this Earth
Functioning as a team with worth!

The multiple connections are amazing!
They work jointly for coordinating.

Because brains are very complicated;
Let us show that they are appreciated!

Yes, our brains benefit from good sleep;
Neurons engage in rapid eye movement.
Deep sleep helps brains do their best;
High performance is in our interest!

A human brain is itself a universe;
Bit tasks require us to rehearse.
Repeated tasks also need practice,
These contributions become positive!

BRAINS HELP US ENGAGE
in COLLABORATING!!

Our bodies are highly complex;
Many components do connect.
Our own central nervous system,
Help us develop or wisdom!

Each body has billions of neurons!
Coordinated by our brain.

These connections do reign;
Experiencing pleasure and pain.

We learn to solve problems;
   So, we can handle challenges.
      These skills are very valuable;
         As our bodies become malleable.

      We very quickly can react;
   To keep our bodies on track!
We learn to do new patterns;
These become vital connections!

Adults help children to learn;
   To develop skills that earn.
      Both on jobs and in school;
         Our brain is a blest jewel!

CONNECTIVITY[2]

Globally the earth is round!
   Like a huge ball can rebound!
      It does not bounce in the universe!
         Circling one direction! Not in reverse!

      The Sun holds the Earth by gravity!
   Each planet held by "Connectivity!"
Earth rotates around the Sun each day!
In a new field called "Connectography!"

---

[2] Khanna, P., 2016, Connectivity: Mapping the Future of Global Civilization, Random House, N.Y.

This new subject succeeds geography!
Moreover, it discourages boundaries!
This whole Earth is seen as globally
Considering this world with integrity!

With everyone together holistically
Global relations done by totality!
This model does include all humanity
The Earth to have a brand, new destiny!

"We" is then the total reference,
Not 'us vs. them" as preference.
National loyalty is discouraged!
"All humanity" to become preferred!

This calls for expanded blending!
Old patriotism comes to an ending!
Nationalism replaced by "Globalism!"
Instead, "One-World" of every citizen!

The globe would not have borders!
Nor divisions due to big rivers!
A cross-borders travel is expected!
Resulting in expanded fluidity!

Of course, changes not immediately!
New developments occur gradually!
Real struggles are to be anticipated!
As "Connectivity" is then developed!

WHY NETWORKING IS ESSENTIAL

Networking has helpful qualities; [3]
It contributes to your activities.
Moreover, it helps your career
It also benefits you hold dear!

Networking involves exchanging ideas!
It broadens your pool of possibilities.
Mutuality becomes a valuable;
Widening your valuable talents.

Long-term relationships may evolve!
You will listen and also contribute!
These may instill to your practices
And your own contacts multiply.

Networking makes you noticeable!
Others discover what is possible!
You also acquire greater visibility
Extending your career flexibility.

You also may find new opportunities,
Discovering fields for your abilities.
Your network extends to new roles;
While relating with more persons.

Time to reassess your qualifications.
Would changing fields for positions?
Good relationships are then advisable,
In order to explore what is now possible!

---

[3] Cole, Bianca M., March 20, 2019, "10 Reasons Why Networking is Essential for Your Career," ForbesWomen.

Your network library may open possibilities;
This helps in match with your abilities!
Your "break-though" might occur
To explore where you can serve!

Some websites address niches;
If you connect where needs arise.
Exploring fields might be very timely;
By searching through these libraries!

Support may come from high profile persons.
They might be available as you explore.
They might open doors now unknown;
You can connect to be then shown!

Your connections can be powerful;
Your search needs to be thorough.
Networking can be very advisable;
This may uncover what is possible.

Networking helps in self-confidence!
You may benefit from providence.
Brushing in your interview skills,
Would be better than more pills!

Relationships can the expand!
As you explore what is new land!
By opening doors, you know more;
To discover what may be in store!

Connecting makes us stronger;
We jointly become tougher!
Collectivity is also enviable;
As this makes us capable.

We then try to be workers;
Together we are even better.
Combining our skills for our tasks,
As co-workers, we hopefully last.

"Be creative to open your connections," [4]
You can imagine what is not there!
Plus, cast your mind to the future,
To encourage other creatures!

See what other persons do not see,
Your vision sees how then to be!
Your creative spark does envision,
What may unfold upon the horizon!

Creativity "sees" what may be new,
This opens doors on what to do!

This helps to make connections;
Writing stories; make inventions.

Life becomes more meaningful! [5]
Preparation is the author's first stage,
Then, secondly, emerges incubation!
"Ideas churn just below consciousness."

The third stage is the phase of insight;
These processes can be a delight!
Then comes processes of evaluation;
To decide what to hold in retention.

Much of creativity is elaboration!
The "blooming" into creation!
The fourth stage takes 99%,
It is worth all the effort!

---

[4] Burns, F., October, 2021, "Free Your Mind," <u>Rotary.</u>

[5] Csikszentmihalyi, M., 1990, <u>Creativity: Flow and the Psychology of Discovery.</u>

IS ANGELOLGY INVISIBLE?

We want to know when and why---
   Answers serve as explanatory.
      Now we seek scientifically;
         Earlier we used "ANGELOLOGY!"

         Angelology was used Biblically; [6]
   Also used to learn historically.
   Then developed scientific methods
Seeking the visible evidences.

Science and Religion compatibility;
   Both benefit to have reliability.
      We hope to think rationally;
         While we also seek reliability.

         Religion and Science are beneficial;
   Yes, we find both very special!
   As humans, we want the truth;
For our allegiances are "COUTH!"

POSITIVE THINKING

During times of contemplating
   Our minds are full of thinking!
      We can usually control thoughts
         Freer thinking has fewer "oughts!"

         Psalms and Paul provide guidance
   Plus sharing with a close partner.
   We do not need and audience
It helps to have an "other!

---

[6] Matthew 26: 51-54 plus other Scriptures.

I Corinthians 13 values "love."
Both partners and God above!
They get us out of the "pits,"
Guiding both thoughts and wits.

Yes, as human "contemplators"
Both in daytime and "nighters;"
Our thought are "delighters"
As contemplations are brighter!

B. PATHWAYS TO MEANING

MEANING for QUALITY of LIVING

Quality living has key meaning!
Characterized what is fulfilling!
Plus, experiences of significance!
That personally have importance!

Meaning makes life worthwhile
Providing a person unique style!
Meaning is internalized within!
Indirectly shown in relating!

Personal autonomy is primary!
Revealed in one's singularity!
Specialness in our personality
No one else has individually!

Even suffering has meaning!
Finding ourselves reflecting!
Life has both joys & sorrows!
Tough time has unhappiness.

Without meaning is a void
As our experiences are bad!
We learn from feeling sad
We can value what is glad!

We become aware of death!
Living helps us feel worth!
Supportive sources do help
Both human & also Divine!

Quality surpasses quantity!
Meaning provides internality!
Inside us is our own depth
Each one's intangibility!

Meaning is not a commodity
It is not bought or sold!
Meaning helps young & old
Valuing us to feel happy!

Each has personal experiences
Providing us with significance!
To God, we each has importance!
Enriching us with essence!

We all possess specialness!
Contributing to our potential!
Discovering is so essential!
Unfolding our uniqueness!

Creative Meaning

Meaning occurs in dimensions of Creativity!
Engaging in actions to express originality.
A new idea that addresses a conundrum
This is valuable at the same time fun!

Yet another opportunity is noticing gaps!
"What's missing?" (this is not a trap)
To perceive what is not even there
This requires imagination to bring it home!

Eyes cannot see something that is missing!
A void" waits to surround a new filling!
A Dentist envisions how to fill gaps!
Thereupon, a new piece is needed perhaps.

New inventions require focused attention!
This may happen within one's imagination.
Perceiving a missing link is creative
Requiring perception for becoming inventive!

Repeating an established pattern is easier;
Discovering a new approach takes creativity.
What was Newton "looking up" to find gravity?
Or Einstein watching to come up with relativity?

These very concepts are present from eternity!
These explanations were derived from theory.
Most new theories require deep thinking
Combining variables to come up to explaining.

Children often "come up" with wild ideas;
Critical feedback can discourage originalities.
They might suppress their unique contributions
And report acceptable ideas, not new inventions.

What are examples of conventional meaning?
Repeating proverbs; old equations repeating!
Like the beginning and ending of the last line
Or quoting just out warn slogans every time!

It is exciting to come up with meaning;
A person is inspired to be gladly exciting!
This affirms the discoverer is special
Their exceptional ideas might be original!

Flexibility facilitates mew creative concepts!
Shifting quickly from old ideas to new precepts!
Rote memory counters creative thinking;
Instead, not processes leads to confirming.

In the past 25-30 years, an emphasis on testing;
Has fallen into the trap of Chinese and Japanese.
Even 50 years ago they saw testing limitations;
However, in recent decades, not American politician.

Children and students decreased in creativeness;
Instead, educators have gone to "testiness!"
How will American students become creative
Instead of doing test that are repetitive?

Major revisions are needed in education;
Businesses and politicians go in wrong directions!
Educational reformation is now essential
For creative students to reach their potential!

MEANING for QUALITY of LIVING

Quality living has key meaning!
Characterized what is fulfilling!
Plus, experiences of significance!
That personally have importance!

Meaning makes life worthwhile
Providing a person unique style!
Meaning is internalized within!
Indirectly shown in relating!

Personal autonomy is primary!
Revealed in one's singularity!
Specialness in our personality
No one else has individually!

Even suffering has meaning!
Finding ourselves reflecting!
Life has both joys & sorrows!
Tough time has unhappiness.

Without meaning is a void
As our experiences are bad!
We learn from feeling sad
We can value what is glad!

We become aware of death!
Living helps us feel worth!
Supportive sources do help
Both human & also Divine!

Quality surpasses quantity!
Meaning provides internality!
Inside us is our own depth
Each one's intangibility!

Meaning is not a commodity
  It is not bought or sold!
  Meaning helps young & old
Valuing us to feel happy!

Each has personal experiences
  Providing us with significance!
  To God, we each has importance!
Enriching us with essence!

We all possess specialness!
  Contributing to our potential!
  Discovering is so essential!
Unfolding our uniqueness!

Creative Meaning

Meaning occurs in dimensions of Creativity!
  Engaging in actions to express originality.
  A new idea that addresses a conundrum
This is valuable at the same time fun!

Yet another opportunity is noticing gaps!
  "What's missing?" (this is not a trap)
  To perceive what is not even there
This requires imagination to bring it home!

Eyes cannot see something that is missing!
  A void" waits to surround a new filling!
  A Dentist envisions how to fill gaps!
Thereupon, a new piece is needed perhaps.

New inventions require focused attention!
This may happen within one's imagination.
Perceiving a missing link is creative
Requiring perception for becoming inventive!

Repeating an established pattern is easier;
Discovering a new approach takes creativity.
What was Newton "looking up" to find gravity?
Or Einstein watching to come up with relativity?

These very concepts are present from eternity!
These explanations were derived from theory.
Most new theories require deep thinking
Combining variables to come up to explaining.

Children often "come up" with wild ideas;
Critical feedback can discourage originalities.
They might suppress their unique contributions
And report acceptable ideas, not new inventions.

What are examples of conventional meaning?
Repeating proverbs; old equations repeating!
Like the beginning and ending of the last line
Or quoting just out warn slogans every time!

It is exciting to come up with meaning;
A person is inspired to be gladly exciting!
This affirms the discoverer is special
Their exceptional ideas might be original!

Flexibility facilitates mew creative concepts!
Shifting quickly from old ideas to new precepts!
Rote memory counters creative thinking;
Instead, not processes leads to confirming.

In the past 25-30 years, an emphasis on testing;
   Has fallen into the trap of Chinese and Japanese.
   Even 50 years ago they saw testing limitations;
However, in recent decades, not American politician.

Children and students decreased in creativeness;
   Instead, educators have gone to "testiness!"
   How will American students become creative
Instead of doing test that are repetitive?

Major revisions are needed in education;
   Businesses and politicians go in wrong directions!
   Educational reformation is now essential
For creative students to reach their potential!

   As an intangible, meaning is elusive.
      It unfolds, then may dissolve and restorable!
         Meaning emerges mysteriously in this world!

   Humans search for personal meaning,
      Pursuing many paths with broad exploring!
         There are positive avenues plus negative exploring!

   First, here an initial positive definition:
      "Meaning emerges when we are pursuing purpose!"
         This involves our discovery of compelling goals in life!

   Plus, positive interpersonal relationships,
      Powerfully promise us with companionship!
         Good connections are facets of partnerships!

   Close interactions include deep sharing,
      Intimacy is powerfully and ideally fulfilling!
         Meaningful experiences are personally revealing!

Healthy involvements can be surprising,
　　Bringing out qualities that likely are hiding!
　　　　Risks come with deep sharing of personal meaning!

Disturbing relationships are dismaying,
　　Loving has capacities for hatred that is puzzling!
　　　　Love and hate are factors symbolically occurring!

Negative experience disturbs meaning,
　　Learning to amend such pursuit is challenging!
　　　　The sorrow of broken relations is part of learning!

Further Pursuits

Let us consider polar opposites,
　　What are characteristics when meaning is absent?
　　　　Meaninglessness feels insignificant and hopeless!

Lack of meaning is depressing,
　　Listless, energy is sapped, life is threatening!
　　　　Sadness happens as personal meaning is missing!

Without meaning a person may feel useless,
　　A corollary is a lack of having genuine purpose!
　　　　Forsaken, abandoned, unnecessary, worthless!

Polar opposites are more positive!
　　Persons feel fulfilled, hopeful & significant!
　　　　Happiness, energized, focused on how to contribute!

Paradox helpfully can be considered!

　　While polar opposites may seem contradictory,
　　　　There may be deeper truths than thinking logically!

Carl Jung's "conuctio oppositorum"[7]
  Provides processes for perceiving truth!
    Truth as each pole can provide us with clues!

MIXED RELATIONS

Our lives as humans are meaningful,
  As we discover activities as purposeful!
    Quality relationships may become powerful!

Abusive relationships are hurtful!
  Exploiting vulnerable persons is painful!
    Negative experiences leave victims feeling shameful!

Divorce and separation are hurtful,
  Spouses and children find separation destructive!
    If one is no longer a "significant other" life is negative!

Violent relations prompt ambivalence,
  These are impulsive human experiences!
    Spouses may not separation but hope for nonviolence!

The probability of positive outcomes,
  Erratic persons involved may readily succumb!
    Despair vies with hopefulness may both exist together!

Children and friends are then often puzzled,
  No wonder participants become very troubled!
    Supportive initial relationships cannot be predictable!

Life encounters joys and sorrows!
  We can be learning from both experiences!
    Optimal balance is beneficial in relationships!

---

[7] Jung, Carl The Collected Works of Carl Jung.

Processes to Re-Discover Meaning

How is a meaningful life created?
Why is this important to live meaningfully?
What are processes for meaning to be discovered?

"Meaningful?" What are key ingredients?
Can these be seen by others who are observers?
When it is possible to recognize it by oneself & others?

What objective clues that can be seen?
Can the subjective experiences be shared?
These additional verses are designed to be explored!

Pursuing clear goals to be engaged!
Meaning is deliberately joyous & purposeful!
Being significant & rewarded by feeling very valued!

A person beams by being recognized!
"I find meaning life as I am important to
Someone who is important to me!" and noticed!

Involvement with others is essential,
Relating to people helps to reach potentials!
Relationships are key in order to be meaningful!

A preliminary definition to consider,
Meaning: "Being reciprocally significant
With referent persons in one's environment!"

Both Nietzsche[8] and Vicktor Frankl [9],
They provided insights in the last century:
"He who has a why to live, can handle any how!"

---

[8] Nietzsche, F.
[9] Frankl, V., Man's Search for Meaning.

CREATION of MEANING

Meaning is created in discovery processes!
Primary sources are other significant persons!
By engaging other people in relationship creatively!

Ultimate meaning is already accessible!
For me, because God values all of His Creation,
Meaning is already here for humans we acknowledge!

Because each person is important to God!
Our meaning is derived by this recognition!
This is our ultimate source of God's own Revelation!

We are personally significant to our Creator!
Because we are valued by each other & our neighbor!
Moreover, we are blessed to possess meaning forever!

Creation has meaning as we are endowed
with inherent worth as a precious gift to be shared!
This multiple meaning for each person is to be valued!

C. SOURCES of MEANING

These activities provide a common bond
Such behaviors are seen as meaningful!
Engaging in actions, laws and theology
By participating, Muslims feel holy!

Islam is considered a noun and verb.[10]
Mohammed is considered a prophet,
Advocated doing, making and acting
For Muslims to be participating.

---

[10] Ahmed, Shahab, 2016, <u>What is Islam?</u> Princeton University Press.

These actions are seen as meaningful!
Plus, practicing behaviors that are helpful!
Over 1.6 billion are considered Muslims
A way of living beyond other religions.

Within Islam are diversity of norms
Sufism, Sunnis, Shiites, Ahmadis.
Plus, Wahhabism as recognized.
As recognized around the global.

Ahmed's writings are a thorough search
The term meaning is used 1000's times.
He lodges personal meaning in Islam
So that Muslim adherents are to find.

In contrast, Christian meaning is to Persons,
Ultimately to the Father, to Holy Spirit, to Son!
We are all important to our Triune God
Meaning is found as He is significant One!

This "Personal Relationship is meaningful!
Bolstered by these concepts as intellectual.
Plus, emotional, graceful and wonderful!
Personal meaning become very powerful!

Ahmed recognizes the search for meaning
It includes loving, believing and trusting.
Human beings understandably are mystified
Searching for God Who is personified.

If you do not know yourself,
Then you cannot know God![11]

---

[11] John, A.H., 1965, <u>The Gift Address to the Spirit,</u> The Prophet, Australian National Spirit.

Initiatives are upon adherents.
Involved in this "Experiment."

Both exegetical analyses are needed;
As well as hermeneutics as applied.
These textual analysis for disclosure
As textual and personal meaningful.

Where are personal relationships?
Between Divine-Human partnership?
Conceptual ideas need supplement
For personal meaning to be definite!

Our linguistic analysis is inadequate!
Meaningfulness thrives in relationships.
Holding relations with a magnet
Involving mutuality personified.

Mohammed received a revelation,
Verbally recorded in The Quran.
How can verbal records reveal
More than words to tell and hear?

Muslims do not call it philosophy;
They recognize it as theology.
Islam is seen as legal conceptions
Recordings of the verbal revelation!

Consequently, Mohammed is a prophet
The Quran states Allah's requirements.
What are relationships thereby derived?
Is The Quran primarily documents?

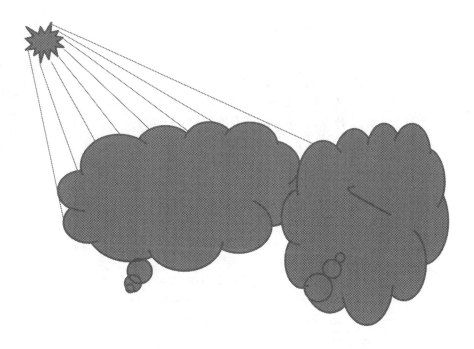

Teaching in India, I searched for shade!
Each tree on my way provided sound aid!
Being near the Equator, it was hot all day!
All year round, the hot sun would stay!

With global temperatures now rising
Researchers for shade are really trying!
Scientific ingenuity is now challenged!
Effective methodologies are being tested!

"Solar geoengineering "tries to slow warming!"
These efforts provide us shades for reaching!
Injection of reflective particles is a technique!
So that the sun rays return out into space!

Even clouds from mountains volcanoes help!
Mt. Pinatubo in the Philippines did a boost!
The Sun's rays did not reach the earth!
But were reflected back into space!

How can the Earth have an umbrella?
Do we have needs for a Cinderella?
Or might we rely upon science?
To help develop clouds to dance!

Clouds flow with wholesome serenity!
Flowing and dancing when it's cloudy!
Cooling the environment for comfort!
Life on Earth would find this of high worth!

II. ADAPTATION TIME4SLINE

Dates of 2050 and 2100 are identified!
How rapidly this Earth is warmed!
To increase 2.5 to 4 degrees C more,
Consensus scientifically is elusive!

Questions arise about living creatures.
What increases can humans tolerate?
How will temperate zones vary?
What areas may be inhabitable?

Many variables are already involved:
How will creatures be habituated?
Previous predictions were inaccurate
Earthly ground and oceans do adapt!

The "Abedo Effect"[12] about ice and snow
They reflect the sun light from below!
Under ice and snow in dark ground
It is Artic carbon erupting around!

Sea level under longer thaws
Could rise 50 meters for awes!
This is faster than Paris Accords!
Threatening cities and sea coasts!

FLOODING

With the global oceans then rising,
The seaports cities will be flooding!

---

[12] Wallase-Wells, D., 2019 The Unihabitable Earth: Life After Warming, Tim Duggan Books, N.Y.

New Orleans, New York City, Houston
Miami and Washington D.C. submerged!

Plus, London, Amsterdam, Stockholm!
Oslo, Copenhagen, Seattle, Portland!
Capetown, Gibraltar, Lyon, Lagos!
Mumbai, Calcutta, Cochin, Chennai!

Singapore, Hong Kong, Tokyo, Shanghai
Jacksonville, Charleston, and Hawaii
San Francisco, Los Angeles, Panama City!
San Paulo, Buenos Aries, Santiago!

Caracas, San Diego, Dublin, Montreal!
Bahamas, Havana, San Salvador,
Vancouver, Accura, Labrador
Lisbon, Rio de Janerio, Lima!

St, Petersburg, Bergen, Halifax
Manilla, Marshall Islands
Brisbane, Jakarta, Archangel
Kuwait City, Corpus Christi!

IMMEDIATELY to INDEFINITELY

As humans, we have limited perspectives:
"Quick! I'm hungry! So, when will we eat?"
Our stomachs have a very short timeline!
When we do not know---we are confined!

How can we look 80 years ahead?
By that time, many will be dead!
Is it our responsibility for posterity?
A century is a timeline for history!

Immediate gratification motivates us!
"Long range forecast? Who can we trust?"
"If we do not eat today! Get out of my way!"
"My aching stomach will not let me play!"

"I do not notice now it is getting hotter!"
Advisories on global warming—"for frogs?"
"Gradual hearing will not cook me!"
"This bubbling kettle is what I see!"

Enough of this old simplistic thinking!
Scientific projections are now providing!
Now here is an image for consideration
Take Washington D.C. capital of nation!

By 2100, the Capitol mall is flooded!
Lincoln Memorial and one for Jefferson!
So, the White House is then under water!
Washington Monument is almost covered!

The Capitol dome is peeking through!
Historical buildings are flooded over!
The Supreme Court now contains fish!
And divers take photos for a dish!

Coastal cities and land all flooded!
Residents have panicked and fled!
Global citizens are facing disasters
Humanity and all life are what matters.

Organizational Development Institute
Offered a study conference in China.
This was an exciting experience
That did capture my interest!

Beijing was our very first meeting;
Tiananmen Square was compelling.
We visited China's Institute of Health.
We also attended a Chinese Opera.

We flew to the ancient capitol, Xian;
The field of Ancient Soldiers nearby.
Constructed over 2000 ago of stone.
They gave realistic impressions.

Chinese food was appreciated
They were all glad that we visited.
Then on to the City of Chunking;
Located high on the Yangtze River

Our Conference was on a Riverboat;
Cruising through the ROYAL GORGES.
We stopped for a day in Wuhan;
Noted now for the coronavirus.

Conferred at Hangzhou University;
I presented a paper on Teamwork!
China had about 200 Psychologists
With keen team-building interests.

Our hosts invited me to do teaching;
So, we made plans for the next year.
A Psychologist was coming to America;
I hosted him on his tour for lectures.

We confirmed plans for the fall of 1989;
I could obtain a new leave-of-absence.
Before the trip, Tiananmen Sq. violence!
Plans were arrested as a consequence.

CONFLICT: Global Warming and "Connectography"

As global warming becomes a reality
    Heating collides with connectography!
        Equatorial people will need to migrate!
            Toward cooler cities they can tolerate!

        Moreover, sea levels are going to rise!
      Coastal cities will have big surprises!
  City populations will move inland!
Searching for jobs & housing to find!

"City Limits" conflict with migration!
    These boundaries "Limit" expression!
      Regulations will increasingly be tested!
        Will these emerging moves be controlled?

        Naturally, there is resistance to change!
    Will migrants be satisfied on the fringe?
  Most will want to be naturally respected
Particularly if they meet that is unexpected!

Borders will seem to be more like barriers!
    Hopefully they will not invade as warriors!
      Flexibility will be so beneficial to everyone!
        So that "the many" coming are welcomed!

        Yes, migrants moving in will test everyone!
    Many changes will not ever become fun!
  Hopefully will be flexible to accommodate
Resulting in respect rather than of hate!

As global warming steadily increases
    Populations will move north & far south

Into both South American and Antarctica
Likewise, upward to Alaska and Siberia!

Permafrost will dangerously thaw out!
Enormous quantity of carbon comes about!
Then much carbon will increase warming!
Humanity searches to demand more cooling!

Conflicts during heat likely will happen!
Violence occurs during high temperatures!
Domestic fighting often also increases
Makes greater demands on police forces!

Conflict management will be tested!
Hopefully this violence will be controlled!
Courts may have their agendas expanded!
Need for justice and peace is learned!

A. COMING TENSIONS

RUSSIA!!!!!!

Russia has a very long history
Launched in the 10th century.

Prince Vladimir from Ukraine
He listened to Mother's advice!

From here awareness of old empires
She knew of empires of Greece and Rome.
Both of them had their very own religions,
Greek Orthodox and Catholic Rome.

Vladimir traveled to Constaninople,
The Orthodox prized leaders' icons.
Catholics valued the Roman Empire
He also admired the Jewish Law.

The Russian Orthodox Church began,
Icons of Saints were then portrayed.
A legend developed to become history
That Russia would be the "Third Rome!"

Initial location was in Valdimir-Suzdal;
A century later moved to Moscow.
Classical Churches were erected
A dome became constructed!

Statues were not formulated;
Iconostatis of historical Saints.
An Iconostatis were erected
This is where Priest served.

Emperors have honored Orthodox;
They assured Churches protection.
A symbolic relation then developed
Kremlin had three Churches erected.

In Orthodox Churches is where you stand
There are no pews upon which to sit.
Worship service may last two hours,
Bread is dipped into the vat of wine.

GLOBAL WARMING

Global warming will produce more conflicts!
Vested economic interests will have fits!

The Earth is changing its environment!
  Tensions will heighten in governments!

  Conservationists like things as they are
  How will they cope both soon and afar?
Environments will dynamically be changed
With higher temperatures people are disturbed!

Aspects of heating are now predictable
  Scientists forecast Disturbing heating cycles!
    Disturbing the living conditions on Earth!
      Some investments will lose their worth!

      The changing conditions are likely coming!
    Weather will transform and be threatening!
Our past conditions will become revised!
Flexibility by people is highly advised!

Major questions about the coming future:
  By 2050, will Europeans migrate to Greenland?
    Then will South Asians try to move to Siberia?
      Will the U.S. citizens migrate into Canada?

      Who will continue to burn coal for energy?
    Will renewable energy replace oil industry?
  Will agriculture produce new ingredients?
Will governments provide creative leaders?

Conservatives are wary of making changes!
  Preferences are very gradually altered!
    Consequently, major questions emerge
      How will conservative begin to cope.

      There are tendencies to blame someone!
    Will conservatives blame the environment?
  Natural developments may not be amenable
Who then to blame for hot temperatures?

Political disputes may be very heated!
Adding to tensions about who is blamed!
Scientific projections provide these warnings
When encountering conservatives for denying!

SUPER INDIVIDUALISM

People in America are on a binge!
By promoting radical individualism!
Self-interests has become dominant
Concern for others suffers negligence!

Global warming needs social attention!
Cooperative efforts done with intention!
Wide teamwork will also be required
Diverse people hope to be protected!

Brooks[13] has "A Declaration of Interdependence!"
Looking onward to more social confidence!
Individual pre-occupation will not be adequate!
Major environmental problems need social efforts!

With global warming, more carbon dioxide!
This stimulates the plants to grow outside!
Those that provide food for nourishment
Will be highly valued with encouragement!

People migrating northward will benefit!
Hopefully this growth will not have limits.
Other animals, birds and insects can thrive
To help all living creatures continue alive!

2018, Alaska's was 20 degrees above normal
Trees move north to release pollen much longer!

---

[13] Brooks, D., 2019, <u>The Second Mountain,</u> Random House, N.Y.

With this infestation of beetles then also comes
Generating contamination with heat from the sun!

Polar bears and reindeer will be displaced!
Snow and ice will disappear; icebergs melted!
Where will geese fly in their summer migration?
What lowlands will be covered by higher sea levels?

Then will walruses continue to even exist?
How about seals wanting to also persist?
Caribou want snow in order to thrive!
Fish want cooler water to stay alive!

What temperatures in the Arctic Circle?
Then imagine living at the North Pole!
This is a long distance from the Equator
The whole Earth may be like an incubator!

Conservatives are wary of changing.
Preferences are very gradually altering!
Consequently, major questions emerging
How will conservatives begin coping?

There are tendencies to blame someone!
Will conservatives blame the environment?
Natural developments may not be amenable
Who then to blame for hot temperatures?

Political disputes may be very heated!
Adding to the tensions who are blamed!
Scientific projections provide these warnings
But encounter conservatives who are denying!

The "El Nino" in the Pacific Ocean,
It is changing without permission!

The Western Hemisphere is influenced!
More rainfall has now resulted!

America has floods more frequently
    This causes crises for Western Hemisphere!
      Moreover, the sea levels are also rising!
        So that sea coasts are now flooding!

        By 2050, Rutgers U. research is reporting
      Sea levels in New Jersey by 2050, 1.4 ft. rising!
    A United Nations Report:[14] Poverty could return!
Particularly as fossil fuels continue to burn!

Poverty could grow for vulnerable persons!
    Obviously for those called Sub-Saharans.
      From 413 million upward to 736 million
        Where is hope for making revisions?

        Also, up to 736 million lacking clean water!
    For many, water will also become saltier!

    Plus 678 million lacking good sanitation!
With most of them living as South Asians!

These projections become more disturbing!
    As verification is included in news reporting!
      Photographic images may become upsetting!
        People may hesitate to report by regretting!

BEFORE and LATER

It is frightening to think of dinosaurs!
    They inhabited the Earth long afar!

---

[14] United Nations Report, 2019.

Then a large asteroid hit this planet!
Causing eruptions into the atmosphere!

Very major changes were consequential!
Many living creatures became terminal!
We now only have fossils as memorable!
Living creatures can become vulnerable!

Humanity can learn about what is possible---
Yes, we all can become very old fossils!
Without ignoring what can be plausible
So, one scenario is that life is fragile!

Yes, living creatures are not eternal!
Life on Earth is known as "temporal!"
Only Divine God is "The Eternal!"
Whose Grace provides an alternable! [15]

This is a "Substitutionary" doctrine in Divinity!
The Earth and humans possess vulnerability!
The Christian Tradition examines this doctrine
Facing the reality of life as approximation!

Facing "alternatives" are among human realities!
Scientific methods recognize probabilities!
Global warming is now timely to research
So that posterity is not left in a lurch!

Dinosaurs did not have these capacities!
However, they left evidence for humanity!
Dinosaurs have left humans with evidence!
Hopefully, life and humanity can now advance!

---

[15] "alter" has 60 variations in <u>Webster's Unabridged Dictionary,</u> "alternable" is one
who takes the place of another.

Yes, posterity will have bases for advancing!
Assuming they're amenable to greater learning!
These capacities will become very invaluable!
As we hopefully desire; they will be capable!

Dinosaurs matter! All creatures matter!
Creation is an opportunity provider!
Validity is inherent for living on Earth!
There is inherent value for our worth!

ONE WAY TO STAY!

Temperate zones may experience surprises!
It may feel much hotter when the sun rises!
Carbon elements will be primary causation
From releases of peat and gaseous explosions!

As ice masses melt, the earth absorbs more!
Sea levels will rise with more height of shores!
Land masses will decrease: less arable land!
Ocean levels rise as the water level expands!

People and animals move to higher ground!
As floods occur; Safe areas need to be found!
Ocean-going ships will need new harbors!
All this travel will require more laborers!

New York City on Long Island will also shrink!
Fortunately, the Statue of Liberty will not sink!
San Francisco Bay cities will also be flooded!
Miami, New Orleans, Seattle are all downers!

The Biblical story of Noah remembered!
Will space ships be further developed?

Launching rockets will add more carbon!
More trees needed to counter this carbon!

Travel to other planets is also very costly!
Moreover, space travel is extremely risky!
There likely would be not return trip!
Going just one-way will likely be it!

Traveling to new worlds is one-way!
If travelers arrive, they will have to stay!
Humans have done this throughout history!
"Out-of-Africa," "Going to the New World to Stay!!

Hopefully, adventurers will be very brave!
Will they consider also living in a cave?
Traveling just one-way is not a rave!
But humans will do it to be ever safe!

Think about the travel of brave pilgrims!
Boarding small ships to reach New England!
Earlier, Columbus with crews boarded ships
Not reaching India: Adventures worth all of it!

In 1969, three Americans reached the moon!
Not to stay, but also equipped to return!
We humans are fascinated with outer-space!
Exploring space is needed by the human race!

B. UNCONSCIOUS MINDS!

There is evidence of our unconscious minds!
It is not readily apparent just how to find!
But our unconscious minds are powerful!
Greater understanding finds it wonderful!

The human body influences our unconscious!
The brain is primary, and so are our senses!
Conscious minds express our awareness!
Our unconscious affects the human race!

Animals possess their own basic instincts
They vary in possessing an intelligence!
Dogs have awareness of human wishes!
Without having their own unconscious!

Humans have a wide range of "intelligences!"
Broader than only academic "awarenesses!"
Social Intelligence understands other people!
Emotional Intelligence senses feelings or others!

Physical Intelligence keen on the body!
Sexual Intelligence knows sexuality!
Team Intelligence helps teamwork!
Weather Intelligence--temperatures work!

Keen people can help train animals!
Audience Intelligence helps good speakers!
Sports Intelligence help build athletes!
Poetry Intelligence is key for the poets!

What are additional intelligences emerging?
These are crucial for humanity surviving!
Adapting to global warming is essential!
For humanity to reach fuller potential!

SHADOWS[16] CONTRIBUTE to CREATIVITY

Our human unconscious is mysterious;
We fortunately can find it serious!
Our collective unconscious, reservoir;
Helps human beings to be superior!

This reservoir is a creative source;
Contributing as a powerful force!
It facilitates our own creativity;
Which is enriched by new ideology!

Creativity benefits from our flexibility;
To incorporate ideas of philosophy!
Deep thoughts are key contributors;
That overcome cautious inhibitors!

Flexibility opens us to new thoughts;
That can often get stuck in rigid ruts1
Our minds can be later pried open;
Beyond old boundaries that stiffened!

MUTLIPLE INTELLIGENCES

Emotional intelligence employs sensitivities!
Personal feelings have vast "intensitivities!"
Recognizing these features is important!
Because people's emotions are significant!

All living beings highly value love!
Among each other and from "Above!"
Mutuality is a very key ingredient!
Respect for love is clearly evident!

---

[16] Jung, C., <u>Unconsious Factpr in Human Personality.</u>

Social relations are built upon trust!
A key phrase to quote: "trust if a must!"
Social Intelligence builds communities!
It is "the glue" that binds our security!

Hyper-connects[17] is now descriptive;
Our association is non-abrasive.
We have numerous connections
This involves our projections!

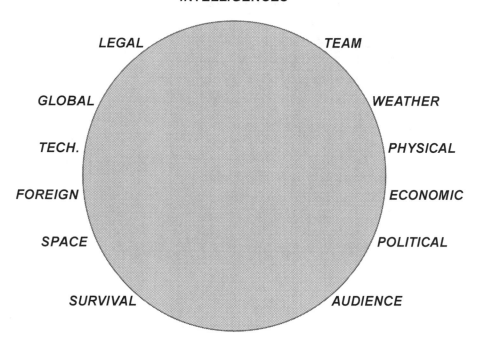

INTELLIGENCES

LEGAL   TEAM

GLOBAL   WEATHER

TECH.   PHYSICAL

FOREIGN   ECONOMIC

SPACE   POLITICAL

SURVIVAL   AUDIENCE

---

[17] Difucio., D., 4/1/22, "Dating Bhemoth sees more human interactions…" <u>Dallas Morning News.</u>

TEMPERATURE

Human sexuality is multi-dimensional
Mutual attraction involves being sexual!
Reproduction for the future is crucial!
Coupling together become every usual!

Families are generated by sexuality!
"Children Begotten" builds up society!
Nurturing "off-spring" is a privilege!
Families perform on the world stage!

Social intelligence generates poetry!
This is a literary gift for humanity!
Poetic literature is a joy to compose!
Poetry is also complementary to prose!

Yes, composing poetry is an art!
Readers and writers are key parts!
Stimulating poems are highly valued!
Participating jointly is what to do!

Musical Intelligence is stimulating!
Whether composing, playing or listening!
Cross-cultural for people and for birds!
Melodies, instrumental or with words!

Faith is complimentary to love and trust!
Placed in God and others is a "must!"
Our hearts, minds and souls are involved!
By discovering faithful mutually in love!

Hope is also trust for a loving future!
Persons who are hopeful feel secure!

Without hope, one's future looks dismal!
These key ingredients aid our survival!

"Peer Intelligence" may sound unusual!
Collegial relations are very valuable!
We join together to combine our efforts!
Leading to a valuable feature of sports!

"Sports Intelligence" demands teamwork!
Playing together involves "reading another!"
Complex tasks require working as a team!
Each person contributes in doing a scheme!

Foreign policy is now also global policy!
These are special disciplined intellectually!
Global cultures are very inclusive!
No one may be considered elusive!

Beyond the Earth is space technology!
In this Universe, it is interplanetary!
The Universe invites our exploration!
This will require large space stations!

Now global warming is a major concern!
The Earth has increasing temperatures!
Ice caps are melting at polar circles!
At this time, no awareness of reversals!

Of course, weather talks are prominent!
Global warming affects all the continents!
Major changes are now gradually happening!
Longitudinal research finds this occurring!

Audience Intelligence may sound strange!
But speakers hope to have a wide range!
This sensitivity to listeners is very crucial!
In order to engage people more than usual!

Speakers need to cultivate their "3rd ear!"
So that they sense what people really hear!
"Listening" involves perceiving their tastes
As hearers do not have more time to waste!

Economics assesses the crowded markets!
Supply and demand balance these reports!
Economics have wide scopes local and global!
The world markets of wants and financials!

Of course, global affairs are also political!
Within every nation and all nations as global!
Decisions are ground out for vast populations!
Hopefully by peaceful means among nations!

Yes, the whole physical world is very involved!
Decisions are implemented after being solved!
Conflicts that arise need effective resolutions!
Because outcomes affect vast populations!

All cultures benefit from legal astuteness!
Laws need to be fair for court effectiveness!
Without civility, the world turns chaotic!
Enhancing needs for courses in civics!

Global warming tests all these disciplines!
In fact, now these are "multi-disciplines!"
Each one has vital contributions to make!
Jointly they have combined places to quake!

Human survival depends upon all of these!
Working together with cooperative ease!
The unknown futures hopefully will unfold!
Both for posterity, the young and the old!

Reliable research contributes to believability!
As humanity needs this help scientifically!
Posterity of the future will be grateful
For contemporary efforts that are helpful!

Timing becomes increasingly important!
To overcome resistance that is reluctant!
Babies born to live in the 22nd century
Will benefit from what is done nowadays!

More clean energy provides vital options!
Foregoing the burning of coal, oil & gas!
For the sake of future generations emerging!
We must make solid efforts to do "cleaning!"

We need to be concerned about future generations!
Hopefully, they too will also enjoy celebrations!
Then they may project far into "beyondering!"
So that future life carries on "projectoring!"

C. HEATING

Life can be in danger when heat is high!
Of course, there is sweating under the sky!
Sweating does help to counter the heat!
Humans and animals may also look beat!

People can suffer from heat strokes, too!
First, they turn red! At death turn blue!
So, caution is in order to keep cooler!
With air conditioning, life is then better!

Shade really helps to hide from the sun!
Children need to be monitored in their fun!

Older persons are also vulnerable to the sun!
Early morning is cooler than the afternoon!

Of course, during the night, the earth is cooler!
Air conditioning classrooms going to school!
So global warming requires more cautions!
Living creatures best limit heavy exertion!

Big trees provide cooler shade from houses!
Moreover, light-colored roofs serve purposes!
Reflecting hot sun rays is recommended!
Along with also having windows shaded!

You already know, we need many clouds
To cover the Earth from the hot sunrays!
Pueblo Indians engaged in rain-dancing!
Tribes did five crucial steps for raining!

Gather Older Men seated in a circle!
Create a fire of wood in the middle!
Have others dance around the big fire!
Rub lightening rocks! Thunder rocks

There are two key conditions in rain-dancing:
One is the crucial faith involves believing!
The 2nd key condition is careful timing!
Finally, everything has to be rhyming!

OK, hopefully readers are humorous!
The topic of global warming is serious!
These pages are to provide you relief!
As we continue onward to real belief!

Heatwaves may become as "Hot as Hell!"[18]
This claim shows that all is not well!

[18] The Economist, July 27, 2019, p. 9.

Human beings need to be prepared!
Be ready to constructively respond!

Heat will become a deadly manifestation!
Deaths become widely dispersed devastations!
In Europe, 2003, 7000 lives were claimed!
By 2040, summers could be commonplace![19]

Often deaths are not attributed to heat strokes!
Temperatures produce lung and heart problems!
All living creatures may be in some danger!
Now constructive preparation to prepare!

Greenland is experiencing global warming!
Its ice sheet has been about two miles thick!
But now it is melting rapidly in this heat!
If it melts, sea levels would rise 24 feet![20]

Deniers claim climate change is a hoax![21]
They are critical of the Paris Agreement!
They claim heating is a current joke!
Media "The Carbon Dioxide Hoax!"

DENIERS and HOAXERS

They claim, kinetic energy is in the Earth!
Mass extinction will begin in about 2060!
Humankind's extinction is Law God made!
America best saves to "Keep America Great!"

---

[19] Britain's Met Office, reported in The Economist, July 27, 2019.

[20] Fountain, H., August 3, 2019, "Air mass That Wilted Europe Moves to Greenland, The New York Times.

[21] Kang, J., & Kanop, J., & M, CO, Ltd., July 24, 2019 in USA Today.

The originators will sell this advertisement!
The copyright price is $20,000,000,000!
"Humankind should not go the same as dinosaurs!"
As people should realize extinction is very near!

Such a sensational claim is being widely printed!
There is not scientific research being claimed!
Careful evaluation is to be highly advised!
This is now seen as an unsubstantiated ad!

Now for a shift to something unusual!
This compresses life on Earth for perusal!
Pre-historic large animals could also return!
As we humorously combine silos and barns!

While traveling in the Upper Midwest in U.S.
Farms are in transition and also unrest!
Cattle barns and silos no longer used!
Standing nobly for farms now passed!

Two suggestions are consequently offered:
One is an artistic example of silos painted!
It now stands as a very tall ear of field corn!
This is an example of "A Silo Reborn!"

There are many 100's of these old silos!
They await being decorated, not eye sores!
Corn is very important grain that nourish!
As many fields of corn currently flourish!

CONNECTING with GOD!

Our God connects with us!
    Expressed by "In God We Trust!"
        Our "Connector" is also our Creator
            As Our God is also our Redeemer!

        Naturally, God is multi-faceted;
    Connecting in numerous dimensions.
    Key facets include the Sciences
As well as our own conscience!

God<>Human connections are reciprocal;
    This faith interaction is also for all!
        Non-verbal communication is clear
            Supplementing our words so dear!

        As humans, we never walk alone!
    God is always going right along!
    Naturally, we also are fortunate
Always with us! There is no wait!

Connecting is our Great Blessing!
    Each day and night is worth living!
        Relating with God provides meaning;
            This helpfully for us is fulfilling!

        Yes, we have connectional Churches;
    Faith in God is a positive connection.
    The Chrisitan Church becomes global;
This responsibility is missional!

        Connectional Church Ministry
        Faith and Fellowship
           Mission Globally

D. PERSONAL MEANING DeMYSTIFIED[22]

We engage by connecting in many ways;
    Of course, in our own social activities.
        Our fields of work make connection;
            As we participate in our professions.

        Learning has many collective processes!
      Most of us connect in the classrooms.
  Classmates engage us in good education;
Great Teachers with student make connection![23]

Teachers so not just sit in front of students;
    Teachers help students make connections!
        They engage with learn other to learn;
            Good questions help this excitement.

        Teachers know student learning styles;
    Each pupil benefit from errors and trials!
Teachers learn to be very observant;
Learning then become more permanent.

So, students and teachers learn together;
    Thus, they helpfully become connectors
        "Eye to Eye" contact is a facilitator,
            Facial expressions help the Teacher.

        During the coronavirus, classes met less;
      Even Zoom connections were not the best.
  These efforts were much better than nothing;
But face-to-face presence is worth doing.

---

[22]   Middents, G., 2018 PERSONAL MEANING DeMYSTIFIED, iUniverse, Bloomington, IN.

[23]   Doggett, J.N., September 1, 2021, "Classrooms are where magic happens, Dallas Morning News.

Likewise, Counseling is better face-to-face,
This facial contact has beneficial presence!
Emotions are thereby more apparent;
These non-verbal ideas are evident.

Counseling becomes very therapeutic;
These processes have a personal magic.
Personal expressions convey connections;
These complement non-verbal articulations.

NETWORKING

Networking is a key human quality;
Practiced by many persons skillfully!
Business people are often networkers;
Cultivating the work skills of co-workers.

Networking is a skill with colleagues;
Communications become dialogues!
It is done locally and globally;
Interacting done with technology.

Contacting with clients is essential;
This key practice is typically vital.
Networking can develop clientele
Helping them know what you sell.

Facebook becomes a helpful tool;
Interacting with others is your pool!
We learn this early in our school,
Then our schedules become full!

CONSCIOUS MEANING and PURPOSE EMERGE

When were aware of your importance?
How do you know your significance?
These processes are key as meaningful!
Humans recognize birth as wonderful.

During pregnancy, parents are "expecting!"
Birth of a child is known as "delivering!"
An infant is not conscious of meaning,
But to parents, new meaning is emerging!

How does a child feel their significance?
Meaning emerges with attention they get!
The young one usually is parents' center!
Parents, siblings, relatives and families!

CONSCIOUS AWARENESS

Consciousness is a special human quality;
It is a very frequent study scientifically! (Gazzinga)
Indicators of awareness are elusive;
Precise measures are inconclusive!

Infants are sensitive to their surroundings!
Watching intently to what they are noticing!
Soon they are aware of someone's absence!
The research studies are done in science.

Infants "learn" how to gain attention!
Crying and fussing is one provision.
Infants notice environmental responses!
As the parents notice these processes!

Siblings are also clearly accessible,
Expanding availability as possible!
"Consciousness" expands in infancy;
Gaining more attention with proficiency!

EXPANDING AWARENESS

Facial recognitions are measurable;
Infants notice familiar faces quickly!
But strange faces can be bewildering!
Immediate reactions include crying!

Experiences with playmates are observable!
From cautiousness to more playful!
The "expansions" contribute to growth
As infants become aware of their "worth!"

Adventurous experiences are valuable;
An Infant's social learning is crucial.
Pre-school activities are facilitators
Careful challenges grow as neighbors!

"GAMES"

Major learning occurs with games!
They contribute how meaning emerges!
The participants do engage one another,
Essential to be teammates or opponents!

Children benefit as participants
Rules of games are be components!

Both sinning and losing make contributions
As meaningful teamwork gives "solutions."

Participants learn both "give and take,"
Game interplay are part of life stakes!
Meaning experiences are an outcome
Helping people to live in "tandem!"

Partnerships become key "by-products!"
These become unanticipated benefits!
Opponents can really be complementary1
Mutual appreciations are exemplary!

Maturation occurs as a child grows up!
Being taller has numerous by-products!
Children are conscious of their height!
Helping to view the taller sights!

Conscious awareness of Our God
Is blessing that becomes valued!
This relationship becomes precious
The highlights in being conscious!

MEANING MULTIPLIES

Consider contributors to a child's meaning;
Parents are unique in a child's growing.
From conception, birth plus rearing!
Mother and Father provide parenting.

A child's siblings are very special!
Sharing exchanges of "give and take!"
Siblings also are closely "reciprocating"
These interactions multiply meanings!

Nurses, "Baby-sitters" and Physicians
Professionally contribute specializations.
Plus, Grandparents, Uncles and Aunts;
Close relationships "expand experiences."

Just as important are their Teachers;
Likewise, are Classmates and Preachers.
Teammates, Coaches, and Bus Drivers!
Plus, other people who are contributors!

BEING IMPORTANT!

Yes, dynamically this may exaggerate
How important egos help to inflate!
Usually a child also has "downers"
Recognizing the room for uppers!

Importance builds child's bodies and souls!
Families, Schools and Religious Institutions.
Also inherently possess very key roles!
Responsibilities as community organizations.

We are all important to Our "Maker!"
"Our Maker" creates us as "Special!"
A recognition is by far unequalled!
So let us rejoice as acknowledged!

BEING MEANINGLESS

To fathom meaning, consider an opposite;
Being without a sense of worth in life!
Existence might become endless strife!
An absence of worth does terrify!

Examples include an abused child.
Beaten by a parent, adult as wild.
Even more repulsive is child neglect;
Humanly abandoned: less than a project!

Dehumanization to less than an animal;
As most species are at least careful!
We then learn to be successful;
Nature makes us colorful!

The haunting eyes and the empty stares!
Immediately suggests that no adult cares!
Fending for food, abused as a person
These gaps are worse than rejection!

STRUGGLING

If an infant survives, what is "it's" future?
Living just as a "thing" without nurture
A helpless child may become a target!
They may be beaten by an angry parent!

Intentional revenge can be acted out
Getting back are a mate turns into hate!
Children symbolically receive hatred;
An upset parent may seek revenge!

A victim of hatred finds this bewildering;
    Bruises, lashes and lack of good nurturing.
        Children may starve physically and emotionally;
            Survival may lead to being lonely and empty!

        Siblings may also become overwhelmed!
      Wartimes conditions when many have died!
    Uncivil parents neglect their own children!
Worse than being jailed or imprisoned!

ANY SCHOOLING?

Abusive and neglectful parents need assistance;
    Schools are unable do this with consistence.
        Such children are victims under bad conditions
            Whole families are in need of education!

        Their Teachers can only meet limited needs;
      If children feel worthless, unable to succeed!
    "Feeling Important" is a facet of meaning;
Children need to be valued for living!

Achieving is crucial to feel important!
    Finding this "road" becomes tantamount!
        "Kids" are naturals to engage in exploration
            So "hunting grounds" become their fixations!

        "Free time" us essential to do exploring!
      Over-control by adults is discouraging.
    Curiosity draws children's adventures
The natural world has wide-open spaces!

PREFERENCES

Children rapidly create their "preferences!"
Creative games can open up entrances!
Girls connect to others and to musicals!
Boys may "rough-house" for their muscles!

Open choices cultivating much creativity!
Too much "structure" inhibits activity!"
Freedom for choices counters formality!
As meaningful actions like spontaneity!

"Look what I made!" needs an audience;
Viewing "What is it?" overcomes chance!
So, "whatever that is?" requires a look
Maybe "what?" is never in a book!

Encouragement is an essential ingredient!
<>Positive Expression!
Meaning
Purpose

♦ Not too Much
○ Not too Little!
▪ But "Just Right!"

WOW!

What are you doing right now?
You will do it better with a "WOW!"
So do not ration your own choices!
Someone benefits among your peers!

When my 1st Granddaughter was born
Her other Grandfather gave his cheers:
"SHE's a Keeper!!!" a very special fish!!!
Nore a tall redhead is quite the dish!

She has become a creative teacher!
In ten years became a "Teacher-Mentor!"
Who is now pursing her Doctorate! "WOW!"
Her achievements do make us very proud!

GROWING

What do we know about growing?
Mostly, what we see is maturing.
Youngsters just seem to be flowing----
Growing---Knowing---Learning!

Girls notice boys who notice girls!
Gender features become apparent!
To girls, boy's behavior seems "icky!"
Boys avoid girls who seen to be picky!

But these distinctions are significant!
Not for the tensions, but meaning!
Subtle messages are readily conveyed,
Behaviors communicate more than words!

Both distinctions and parallel interests!
Like their DNA and RNA spiral around!
Parents, Teachers, and friends see more;
Hoping positive futures are in store!

SEXUALITY

Species depend upon their sexuality;
  Relationships may often become erratic!
    Fortunately, species thrive prolifically.
      Handling these challenging dynamics!

      Becoming important to one another
    Overcomes obstacles to be prolific!
  Powerful attractions do predominate;
Failing pairs go through "love-hate."

Cultural variances are distinctive!
  Ceremonies express precious meaning!
    These "promise-making commitments"
      Are expressing positive sentiments.

      Mental and physical health evolves;
    Timely care and what this involves!
  Persons both thrive and also neglect;
Essential care of health they protect!

These life challenges require mastery;
  Persons need "hope to cope" or suicide;
    Meaningful relationships are vital,
      Undergirding persons to confide!

      Being significant to others is imminent;
    Living ahead is affirmed as worthwhile.
  Current thriving into new future styles
Bolsters persons to face life and its trials!

RESILIENCE!

Bouncing Back!
Back on Track!
Ever Healthier!
Mentally Tougher!
Positive Responses!
Restorative Bounces!
By Living Positively!
Recovering Resiliently!

Forging Ahead!
Upward Lifts!
Moving Forward!
Future Hopeful!
Loving Holding!
Sharing<>Daring!

SO MUCH!

Young people experience so much!
New thoughts; New pains; a Bunch!
Future hopes yet to become known;
Much more than talking on a phone!

Images influence inner thoughts;
Imagining both what is and "oughts!"
Who will be my friends? My mate?
So why do I have to now wait?

New living without past history;
Life unfolds just life a mystery!
What will I be doing next year?
Will living be happy or full of fear?

Why can't I know this right now?
OK! I am not God! I'm in the flow!
Yes, life progresses a day at a time
But knowing now would be sublime1

As youth are expected to be ready;
Not aware if life will be steady.
Who will become my mate?
Might be someone I date?

And what work will I have?
Will I earn enough I can save>|?
Where might we decide to live?
Will we be fortunate to thrive?

OK, life unfolds one day at a time;
Will I work? Be married to "mine?"
These questions may flood my curiosity!
Is living slow or speedy in velocity?

PONDERINGS

Will my life always be full of ponderings?
Young persons may fin questions flooding!
Is this typical for others who are now existing?
How can I be ready? what could I be missing?

Let us be thankful to be more than animals!
They do not ponder at even a minimal!
As humans, we deal with complexities;
It is natural to have these uncertainties!

Maybe it is best to consult and confer!
Experienced advice is readily available.

Trustworthy adults and also Ministers;
Along with our Parents and our Teachers.

VOLUNTEERING

Wonderful skills come with networking;
Often developed when volunteering.
Volunteers off their service for free;
They contribute without any fee!

The Peace Corps relies on volunteers;
They readily influence their peers.
Their willing services are contagious,
Their relationships are also gracious.

Over 241,000 have already served!
Their dreams may then be fulfilled!
Beneficiaries typically are grateful,
All who are involved feel mutual.

Rotary International is done by volunteers;
This organization is for over 100 years.
"If you dream it, you can do it!"[24]
Ideas are planted to become a hit!

My personal experiences do concur.
Volunteering to teach at Mahatma Gandhi U.
Then three years later at Manipal University
In order to fill the UNESCO Peace Chair.

---

[24] Germ, J.F., Sept. 2021, "The Rotary Foundation Chair," ROTARY mangazene.

"SERVICE is the RENT we pay for Space we Occupy on Earth!"[25]

The Organizational Development Institute
It was a professional group I belonged.
It did provide global connections
As a professional organization.

One conference was in Nepal;
So, Carol and I also visited India.
We then had three trips to India,
I presented a professional paper.

Previously, we had met in China;
At the University of Hangzhou.

My program was on teamwork
I was invited to teach in 1989!

Beijing Square violence interfered.
This was a great disappointment!
I did host a Chinese Professor,
But he was not a "connector."

This Organization met in Europe;
Yugoslavia is where we met.
My program caught attention,
It was followed with an invitation.

This was to Ljubljana University;
But Yugoslavia fell into disunity.
Again, this invitation fell through
Internationally, it would not do.

---

[25] Mehta, S., October, 2021, <u>ROTARY,</u> One Rotary Center, 1560 Sherman, Ave., Evanston, Ill. 60201.

I hosted a Marxist Economist;
It was my pleasure to persist.
My colleagues were impressed;
This illustrated being connected.

BEING a CONNECTOR

A special role is becoming a connector!
Being actively involved; not a spectator.
This is a role that needs an activator!
Best to engage, sooner not later!

Rotarians connect locally and globally;
As, Service is our motto for loyalty.
Key projects gain our attention.
We reach out as extensions.

Yes, this involves being in the middle;
Many occasions benefit by being able.
As a connector, one is a key facilitator;
By trying to act as a problem-solver!!

Our "vestibular" facilitates our balance;
It is located near our hearing mechanism.
With delicate hairs lodged in sensing fluid
We can walk erect with our head high.

Yes, our vestibular counters gravity;
Gravity pulls us securely to the Earth.
Fortunately, it works in our development
So that we are able to keep our balance.

FOOD

Living creatures need food;
  We want meals that are good!
    Our food needs to nourishing
      Plus, what we enjoy cooking.

      Various cultures have favorite foods.
      Consider what you already approve.
    We eventually learn to love,
Their quality fit like a glove!

In India four times totaling a years
  Conditioned me to select specialties.
    I like their lentils and chick peas.
      Plus, very light sprinkles of curry!

      Many European nations have specialties:
      Borsch>Russia, Wurst>Germany>Pizza in Italy!
    Cheese in Switzerland; Dumpling in Poland.
Mousaka in Greece; Meatballs in Sweden.

CONNECTING with ANCESTORS

We can connect with family records;
  We are descendant of our ancestors.
    They are our family predecessors,
      Because we are their inheritors.

      Naturally, most are no longer living,
      But, we are indebted to them for being.
    We likely will observe many of our features,
We are the ones to carry forward their genes.

Our own descendants will find these helpful,
So then, we need to become very careful.
They will likely see us as connectors,
As they in time will move forward.

Very likely, descendants are curious;
As they appreciate past and futures.
Photographs and video tapes do help;
For them to appreciate their forebearers.

WAYS to be a RECONNECTOR

Coupling does have multiple meanings;
These are dynamics for connectings;
Couples together are "matings;"
Connect in processes of dating.

Coupling is a process for mates;
By-sexually and also same sex.
All species have mates coupling;
Rarely are cross-species relating.

Each partner attracts the other;
Jointly, they become partners.
This involves powerful processes;
Both emotionally and physically.

Living creatures exemplify coupling,
Outcomes may involve reproducing!
Cultures value the resulting outcomes;
As theses sequences have consequences.

"Coupling" is also used when building;
Carpenters join parts by coupling.

They are also known as "joiners;"
　Housing structures connectors.

　This world values large structures;
　Skyscrapers reach multiple stories!
　The tallest now is in the Middle East;
In cultures for whom oil has increased.

Farmers and ranchers use couplings;
　Holding together diverse parts.
　Connecting vast structures;
　　With many configurations.

III. INTER-CONNECTING the SOLAR SYSTEM

Gravity of the Sun is powerful;
Holding planets in their orbits!
The Earth circles around the Sun
Over five billion Stars begun!

Mercury and Venus nearer the Sun
Their temperatures are even hotter!
Mars is further than the Earth
Uranus has a larger girth.

Stars are far away in the Sky;
Telescopes provide closer views.
Stars have their circling planets,
We wonder if they have life, too.

There may exist multi-verses!
These expand our awareness.
We exist with many unknowns;
Awaiting what may be shown.

The Universe stimulates curiosity;
It is hold together by gravity.
This vastness merits respect;
Vastness is what we expect

GLOBAL WARMING

We humans are in need of learning;
Carbon consumption<>global warming!

Yes, what we process when consuming;
It is significant to make "connecting!"

How might we make right decisions?
So that we make these connections?
We are consuming carbon gases;
In our vehicles and our factories!

As a result, the Earth is warming;
To the Paris Agreement violating.
In the Industrial Age we are changing;
In manufacturing and in our farming.

Our practices need to be controlled;
These patterns hopefully reversed
Earthly carbons do contribute
Humans must stop this abuse!

Our sources of power must change;
Instead of carbons, use the alternatives.
Wind power is one source to improve;
Plus, solar energy is another available.

CONNECTING in BASEBALL

Special terminology in baseball
Is then applied when at bat
When a batter gets a hit
"Connecting is called it!

"Single" gets a batter to first;
"Double" gets a batter to second;
"Triple" gets a batter to third;
A "home run becomes a score.

Pitchers try to get "strike outs!"
Three outs retire opponents!
Defensive fielders catch "flies,"
Defenders stop the grounders!

Three "outs" retires the offense;
A typical game is nine innings.
And if teams are then tied,
Extra innings are played!

ROTARY CONNECTS US TOGETHER

Rotary International connects,
To undertake many projects!
Rotary's scope is international
This is supported as factual!

All ages are benefited,
All cultures are included!
Projects are world-wide
Rotarians are on your side.

Now as a member foe 45 years;
Served four global projects.
In India for three times
Nicaragua 4th rhymes.

Rotary seeks global peace!
Balanced by social justice!
You can serve as a Rotarian
Helping you be a Good Samaritan!

CONNECTING vs. CONTROLLING

Many humans want to control,
Particularly those who are bold.
Connecting has risks for them;
They want to know how and when.

Of course, control is important;
But connecting is also significant.
We develop good connections;
That become our fine relations.

Relationships may be supportive,
They also become collaborative!
Together, we become creative;
An outcome of being connective.

Creativity is constructive responses;
Including flexibility and also fluency.
Originality is a key in our creativity;
We may engage in these activities daily.

My writing focuses on "connecting,"
This poetry expands our sharing.
We belong to a very big flock
As we are part of this stock!

Yes, we also gather together;
Like birds with lovely feathers.
As Jesus' followers, we gather
To address issues that matter.

Yes, we sing to beautiful music;
Plus, we are glad to share it!

Music is good for our well-being;[26]
It also is helpful for healing.

ISOLATIONISM<>CONNECTIONISM

America had a history of isolation;
Geographical distant from Europeans;
Limited 13 states sought independence;
From colonial powers expectations.

This initial history of isolationism,
Influenced many U.S. decisions.
Oceans kept America apart
Our nation at its own start.

Developments brought connections;
Population grew by immigration;
Many immigrants were Europeans
Mixing up U.S. diversification.

Immigrants became Americans;
This naturally brought tensions.
This nation had isolation
Geographical plus intention.

But connections are powerful;
Relatives vs. isolationism!
Different loyalties are involved;
Enriching and also troubled.

Some stresses become creative;
Bad tensions are destructive.
Value the best as constructive;
As results of these connectives.

---

26 Middents, G., 2021, <u>Asounding Music,</u> iUniverse Press.

A. CONNECTING with VOTERS

Politicians who connect with voters
   Know that the voters are deciders!
      Winners then serve in office
         To vote on issues to decide.

      In elections decided by voters
      Candidates want to be winners.
   Voting is a major key responsibility
This vote is vital in any democracy.

"Voting is for the people, by the people;"
   Each voters' vote is considered equal.
      Voters need to become informed
         About issues and candidates.

      Democracies make vital demands
      More than spectators in the stands.
   Fans may cheer loudly for favorites
But voters are responsible to candidates.

I have been active in ten campaigns;
   My son served as a Judge in Texas.
      First, there are primary campaigns,
         Political parties each have candidates.

      My Son won in nine elections;
   He served for 16 years in Texas!
In 2008, the opposition prevailed;
Then He became a Juvenile Officer.

He is a dedicated public servant,
   Now serving Biden's Administration.
      He had helped in Biden's election
         As this is a role in this nation.

The voting public has a vital role!
Deciding how to make their vote.
Media also has a very key role,
Both print and broadcast help.

ECONOMIC CONNECTIONS

Supply and Demand are key factors;
These elements are connectors!
If the supply exceeds the demand,
Prices will typically increase!

Contrary dynamics can reverse;
If demand every does increase,
The prices typically will be higher.
Thereby, these dynamics will occur.

Manufacturers watch the market closely,
Producing what will sell very quickly.
Consumers also watch is on sale,
Realizing when time to buy.

Demand by buyers does indicate,
When to purchase at that date.
As buyers and sellers do relate
Producers watch what to create.

QUESTIONS

Asking constructive questions
Is crucial in our education.
This is how humans learn.

Effective teachers ask questions,
Guiding students for directions.
Putting brains into motions!

Questions<>Answers connect!
Theses combinations interact.
By making our brains react!

What? How? When? Why?
Questions needing a reply!
Processes used scientifically.

Questions then are very vital;
Lawyers design them for trials.
Good inquiries are so vital!

TOGETHER

Most humans join together
For support and pleasure!
We congregate to be better
Joining is the best measure!

We formulate into societies;
Like ants form colonies.
People create their families;
Nations combat enemies.

Apart we become lonely;
Isolation feels horribly.
We join into organizations
We also establish nations!

Yes, we make many connections
Valuing our human relations.

Jointly we are also healthier
Together, we are sturdier!

ASSERTION

In order to be connective;
One has to be assertive.
This is a human way
To have a better day!

Valuing our human rights
Displaying non-violence.
This is not passivity
But showing creativity.

Yes, Jesus was assertive!
Yes, he was decisive!
Mahatma Gandhi of India,
M.L. King from America!

I also taught non-violence,
And concepts of assertiveness.
This subject was a witness
Including non-violence!

Power is an elusive human expression!
Expressed excessively or with discretion!
How do human use power appropriately!
So that that power is expressed ethically?

History reveals the fitting & abusive!
Difficult to assess as human motives!
Controls may be present or absent!
In order to set appropriate limits!

Human reactions are unpredictable!
Under pressure & threat inexplicable!
Most persons recognize this problem!
In addressing what to recommend!

This literary piece has hesitation
The writer gives varied recognition!
With trepidation and hopefulness
Let us proceed with carefulness!

TEAM DISRUPTION

Effective teams seek cooperation;
Improving their team production!
Tension may result in disruption
And this may lead to corruption.

Power by humans is ambiguous!
Used unconsciously and conscious!
Power may be open or disguised!
Often power is used by surprise!

Authority figures express power!
Parents control those younger!
Teachers use class discipline!
Police control criminal and victims!

Adults may be abusive to children!
Spouses may control their mates!
Police can arrest the suspicious!
Robbers may become malicious!

RECOGNIZING AGGRESSION

Bullying can be done openly
　　Picking victims quite instantly!
　　　Some victims prompt bullying!
　　　　Bully-victim make a "Pairing!"

Bosses have major responsibilities!
　　Then subordinates become utilities!
　　　Government leaders have authority!
　　　　Governing people in their citizenry!

Assumptions see power consciously!
　　Abuses may be done unconsciously!
　　　Neither party may have awareness!
　　　　Until abuses become obvious messes!

Professionals may overwhelm clients!
　　Physicians may over-control patients!
　　　Clergy may serve as if they are God!
　　　　Judges may make their rulings weird!

DIS-CONNECTING

Russia is losing their connections;
　　Bombing Ukraine by destruction.
　　　Putin made some bad decisions;
　　　　Other nations have many questions.

　　　Peaceful countries promote justice;
　　They engage in healthy practices.
　　Most take steps to engage in trade;
Their citizens will extend their aid.

Disconnecting prompts questions;
Separating raises defensive emotions.
Businesses may neither buy nor sell;
The fragile ones will often fail.

Disconnecting results in distrust;
Investors are unable to build wealth.
Inventions may not be developed;
New technology may also be stifled.

WHAT ARE ABUSES of POWER?

Is capital punishment abusive?
Debate now continues as useful!
What is bases for death sentences?
Can humans decide without biases?

Do humans have rights for guns?
Is it provided in 2nd amendment?
To bear arms as a personal right?
Only intended for national defense?

How can Presidents legally initiate war?
Or does Congress serve as the "Decider?"
After WW II, has this been abused?
Consider how this power is used!

Korean War had no Congressional approval!
Over 50,000 American casualties resulted!
Plus, Vietnam was the "American War!"
Bay of Tonkin Resolutions undeclared!

Are these abuses or are they neglect?
Is Combat against ISIS ever correct?

Obama seeks Congressional approval!
To declare war limited to three years!

Ambiguity continues for starting wars!
When invasions do occur, it is clearer!
Attacks by any terrorists is a puzzle!
No nation is considered as terrorists!

V-P Cheney was CEO of Haliburton!
Insiders 2001-9, this was uncertain!
Private contractors are "only for profit!"
This arrangement does not deserve credit!

Protestant traditions emphasize detecting errors,
Reducing originality insistent on historic connections.
Shifting ideas through old filters reduced imagination,
New ideas deconstructed using historic assumptions.

Western religions tend to codify proper behaviors,
Thereby contradicting gracious mercy of God's Love.
Trusting faith is central in Christian doctrinal beliefs,
This is often delivered by emphasizing judgments!

Eastern traditions mix conformity as well as creativity,
Being less legalistic in both writings and applications.
While the East is more tribal, the West stresses freedom,
Codified doctrines with prescribed practices of serfdom!

Legalistic codes restrict freedom for new expressions,
Stifling creative stories while avoiding original ideas!
Creative thinking is constrained within severe limits,
Within criterion of precedence already established.

By 2014, estimate $1.7 trillion expended!
Cost of victims' care is not even included!
Economists estimate $3 trillion overall
What can justify this pre-emptive war?

Pre-emption is seen as not being attacked!
But speculation pre-emptors might act!
Pre-emptors take initiative before attack!
What justifies preliminary war action?

MORE AMBIGUITY

Reagan, 1983, had Congressional approval
But actual war in Lebanon did not occur
His invasion of Grenada not acted upon!
1991 attack on Iraq for occupying Kuwait!

No Congressional declaration in 1991
To invade and occupy Afghanistan!
In 2003, Bush/Cheney beyond Congress
Invaded Iraq so two wars were pursued!

GOVERNMENTS

Political leaders can abuse authority!
Unaware they can act unconsciously!
Presidents, Royalties, Dictators
May not be recognized as abusers!

America's three branches of government!
Serving to balance power of their offices!
Examples of abuse are very numerous!
Pretending as civil servants is dubious!

Congress may control or neglect!
Legislative proposals as their acts!

Supreme Courts may act like God!
Presidents may wield power as a rod!

Governments may engage in war!
Identifying enemies to slaughter!
These aggressive actions can occur!
To overwhelm enemies as others!

WEALTH

Superiority deceives many wealthy
That they should dominate lowly!
Unequal power is exerted frequently!
By leading poor persons into slavery!

Control is assumed by the wealthy!
Tempting them to dominate cruelly!
Justice often favors the controllers
Stifling the lives of those poorer!

Money is abused by many as power!
Rather than a resource as sharers!
Passing on the wealth to inheritors
Perpetuates inequities to successors!

Assumption of power is contagious!
Frequently this is very unconscious!
This can result in serious injustice!
Social problems can become a mess!

PASSIVE USE of POWER

Ignoring problems becomes passive!
　Not recognizing what are injustices!
　　When citizens do not become active
　　　Persons may not know how to live!

Passive aggression is very slippery!
　But adolescents learn this quickly!
　　Agree with the authority figures
　　　Then do not comply as actors!

People who utilize nonviolence
　Misunderstood as being passive!
　　But nonviolence can be very active!
　　　Defeating those who are aggressive!

When controlled by aggression
　Different tactics for one's actions!
　　Direct opposition is not warranted
　　　While discipline is recommended!

APPROPRIATE USE of POWER

This topic is very challenging!
　How not to become controlling!
　　Fighting back is not recommended
　　　It results in more violence un-ended!

Violence results in more violence!
　A vicious cycle has continuance!
　　How can humans live peacefully?
　　　By living together respectfully!

Between aggression and passivity
Is "ASSERTIVENESS" as priority!
Asserting our own personal rights
Without violating others' rights!

Assertiveness requires discipline
Controlling one's own reactions
This undoes aggressive actions
By not responding with aggression!

PRACTICES

Instead of accusing other persons
Who often state: "You" accusations!
Reply with one's own responses
"I..." rather than accusatory "You...."

Being in touch with oneself
Helps self-control as ourselves!
Attacking aggressors is unworkable!
This soon heightened confrontations!

Assertiveness stands for one's rights!
Undoing the aggressor's own attacks!
After practice, these are effective
Appropriate and also expressive!

Countering aggression is recommended
Plus, passive-aggression as practiced!
Assertiveness needs personal discipline
To become effective and also responsive!

B. ASSERTIVE POWER!

Power is an elusive human expression!
Expressed excessively or with discretion!
How do human use power appropriately!
So that that power is expressed ethically?

History reveals the fitting and abusive!
Difficult to assess as human motives!
Controls may be present or absent!
In order to set appropriate limits!

Human reactions are unpredictable!
Under pressure & threat inexplicable!
Most persons recognize this problem!
In addressing what to recommend!

This literary piece has hesitation
The writer gives varied recognition!
With trepidation and hopefulness
Let us proceed with carefulness!

ASSERTION

In order to be connective;
One has to be assertive.
This is a human way
To have a better day!

Valuing our human rights
Displaying non-violence.
This is not passivity
But showing creativity.

Yes, Jesus was assertive!
Yes, he was decisive!
Mahatma Gandhi of India,
M.L. King from America!

I also taught non-violence,
And concepts of assertiveness.
This subject was a witness
Including non-violence!

Power is an elusive human expression!
Expressed excessively or with discretion!
How do human use power appropriately!
So that that power is expressed ethically?

History reveals the fitting & abusive!
Difficult to assess as human motives!
Controls may be present or absent!
In order to set appropriate limits!

Human reactions are unpredictable!
Under pressure & threat inexplicable!
Most persons recognize this problem!
In addressing what to recommend!

This literary piece has hesitation
The writer gives varied recognition!
With trepidation and hopefulness
Let us proceed with carefulness!

TEAM DISRUPTION

Effective teams seek cooperation;
Improving their team production!

Tension may result in disruption
And this may lead to corruption.

Power by humans is ambiguous!
Used unconsciously and conscious!
Power may be open or disguised!
Often power is used by surprise!

Authority figures express power!
Parents control those younger!
Teachers use class discipline!
Police control criminal and victims!

Adults may be abusive to children!
Spouses may control their mates!
Police can arrest the suspicious!
Robbers may become malicious!

RECOGNIZING AGGRESSION

Bullying can be done openly
Picking victims quite instantly!
Some victims prompt bullying!
Bully-victim make a "Pairing!"

Bosses have major responsibilities!
Then subordinates become utilities!
Government leaders have authority!
Governing people in their citizenry!

Assumptions see power consciously!
Abuses may be done unconsciously!
Neither party may have awareness!
Until abuses become obvious messes!

Professionals may overwhelm clients!
Physicians may over-control patients!
Clergy may serve as if they are God!
Judges may make their rulings weird!

WHAT ARE ABUSES of POWER?

Is capital punishment abusive?
Debate now continues as useful!
What is bases for death sentences?
Can humans decide without biases?

Do humans have rights for guns?
Is it provided in 2nd amendment?
To bear arms as a personal right?
Only intended for national defense?

How can Presidents legally initiate war?
Or does Congress serve as the "Decider?"
After WW II, has this been abused?
Consider how this power is used!

Korean War had no Congressional approval!
Over 50,000 American casualties resulted!
Plus, Vietnam was the "American War!"
Bay of Tonkin Resolutions undeclared!

Are these abuses or are they neglect?
Is Combat against ISIS ever correct?
Obama seeks Congressional approval!
To declare war limited to three years!

Ambiguity continues for starting wars!
When invasions do occur, it is clearer!

Attacks by any terrorists is a puzzle!
No nation is considered as terrorists!

V-P Cheney was CEO of Haliburton!
Insiders 2001-9, this was uncertain!
Private contractors are "only for profit!"
This arrangement does not deserve credit!

Protestant traditions emphasize detecting errors,
Reducing originality insistent on historic connections.
Shifting ideas through old filters reduced imagination,
New ideas deconstructed using historic assumptions.

Western religions tend to codify proper behaviors,
Thereby contradicting gracious mercy of God's Love.
Trusting faith is central in Christian doctrinal beliefs,
This is often delivered by emphasizing judgments!

Eastern traditions mix conformity as well as creativity,
Being less legalistic in both writings and applications.
While the East is more tribal, the West stresses freedom,
Codified doctrines with prescribed practices of serfdom!

Legalistic codes restrict freedom for new expressions,
Stifling creative stories while avoiding original ideas!
Creative thinking is constrained within severe limits,
Within criterion of precedence already established.

By 2014, estimate $1.7 trillion expended!
Cost of victims' care is not even included!
Economists estimate $3 trillion overall
What can justify this pre-emptive war?

Pre-emption is seen as not being attacked!
But speculation pre-emptors might act!

Pre-emptors take initiative before attack!
What justifies preliminary war action?

MORE AMBIGUITY

Reagan, 1983, had Congressional approval
But actual war in Lebanon did not occur
His invasion of Grenada not acted upon!
1991 attack on Iraq for occupying Kuwait!

No Congressional declaration in 1991
To invade and occupy Afghanistan!
In 2003, Bush/Cheney beyond Congress
Invaded Iraq so two wars were pursued!

GOVERNMENTS

Political leaders can abuse authority!
Unaware they can act unconsciously!
Presidents, Royalties, Dictators
May not be recognized as abusers!

America's three branches of government!
Serving to balance power of their offices!
Examples of abuse are very numerous!
Pretending as civil servants is dubious!

Congress may control or neglect!
Legislative proposals as their acts!
Supreme Courts may act like God!
Presidents may wield power as a rod!

Governments may engage in war!
Identifying enemies to slaughter!
These aggressive actions can occur!
To overwhelm enemies as others!

WEALTH

Superiority deceives many wealthy
That they should dominate lowly!
Unequal power is exerted frequently!
By leading poor persons into slavery!

Control is assumed by the wealthy!
Tempting them to dominate cruelly!
Justice often favors the controllers
Stifling the lives of those poorer!

Money is abused by many as power!
Rather than a resource as sharers!
Passing on the wealth to inheritors
Perpetuates inequities to successors!

Assumption of power is contagious!
Frequently this is very unconscious!
This can result in serious injustice!
Social problems can become a mess!

PASSIVE USE of POWER

Ignoring problems becomes passive!
Not recognizing what are injustices!
When citizens do not become active
Persons may not know how to live!

Passive aggression is very slippery!
But adolescents learn this quickly!
Agree with the authority figures
Then do not comply as actors!

People who utilize nonviolence
Misunderstood as being passive!
But nonviolence can be very active!
Defeating those who are aggressive!

When controlled by aggression
Different tactics for one's actions!
Direct opposition is not warranted
While discipline is recommended!

APPROPRIATE USE of POWER

This topic is very challenging!
How not to become controlling!
Fighting back is not recommended
It results in more violence un-ended!

Violence results in more violence!
A vicious cycle has continuance!
How can humans live peacefully?
By living together respectfully!

Between aggression and passivity
Is "ASSERTIVENESS" as priority!
Asserting our own personal rights
Without violating others' rights!

Assertiveness requires discipline
Controlling one's own reactions

This undoes aggressive actions
By not responding with aggression!

PRACTICES

Instead of accusing other persons
Who often state: "You" accusations!
Reply with one's own responses
"I..." rather than accusatory "You...."

Being in touch with oneself
Helps self-control as ourselves!
Attacking aggressors is unworkable!
This soon heightened confrontations!

Assertiveness stands for one's rights!
Undoing the aggressor's own attacks!
After practice, these are effective
Appropriate and also expressive!

Countering aggression is recommended
Plus, passive-aggression as practiced!
Assertiveness needs personal discipline
To become effective and also responsive!

DIS-CONNECTING

Opposite concepts do occur;
Their outcomes ae not sure.
These occasions catch attention
Disconnecting has apprehension.

Marriages can end by divorce;
Tensions are present, of course.
Legal separation then occurs,
Such disconnection closes doors.

Children are then directly affected;
Disaffection of parents has occurred.
The couples' bond of love is broken
Unkind words are often spoken.

Terminating marriage has consequences;
Perhaps some relief in many instances.
Any angry emotions maybe severed;
Once lovers! But now separated.

Divorce results in termination;
Of marital status; not parenthood.
Children have their own loyalties
They try, but have discontinuities.

Separation has its limitations;
Human beings avoid separation.
We often want to be together
By joining, we live better.

Persons thrive by connecting;
Together is our way of working.
Jointly may result in thriving;
This results many are hoping.

AGGRESSIVE USE of POWER

Unconscious use & abuse or power
Contrasting with conscious users!

Often aggression can be spontaneous
Used without balancing impulsiveness!

Power by humans is ambiguous!
Used unconsciously & conscious!
Power may be open or disguised!
Often power is used by surprise!

Authority figures express power!
Parents control those younger!
Teachers use class discipline!
Police control criminal & victim!

Adults may be abusive to children!
Spouses may control their mates!
Police can arrest the suspicious!
Robbers may become malicious!

RECOGNIZING AGGRESSION

Bullying can be done openly
Picking victims quite instantly!
Some victims prompt bullying!
Bully-victim make a "Pairing!"

Bosses have major responsibilities!
Then subordinates become utilities!
Government leaders have authority!
Governing people in their citizenry!

Assumptions see power consciously!
Abuses may be done unconsciously!
Neither party may have awareness!
Until abuses become obvious messes!

Professionals may overwhelm clients!
Physicians may over-control patients!
Clergy may serve as if they are God!
Judges may make their rulings weird!

WHAT ARE ABUSES of POWER?

Is capital punishment abusive?
Debate now continues as useful!
What is bases for death sentences?
Can humans decide without biases?

Do humans have rights for guns?
Is it provided in 2nd amendment?
To bear arms as a personal right?
Only intended for national defense?

How can Presidents legally initiate war?
Or does Congress serve as the "Decider?"
After WW II, has this been abused?
Consider how this power is used!

Korean War had no Congressional approval!
Over 50,000 American casualties resulted!
Plus, Vietnam was the "American War!"
Bay of Tonkin Resolutions undeclared!

Are these abuses or are they neglect?
Is Combat against ISIS ever correct?
Obama seeks Congressional approval!
To declare war limited to three years!

Ambiguity continues for starting wars!
When invasions do occur, it is clearer!

Attacks by any terrorists is a puzzle!
No nation is considered as terrorists!

WHAT IS OUR DUTY?

Soldiers report to duty in uniform!
U.S. is defended by men and women!
Soldiers will obey as their orders!
Defending U.S. interests or borders!

Volunteers have not been enough!
Without a draft, this is very tough!
So "private contractors" do bidding!
Private authority, not military drilling!

But contracting has become abusive!
Haliburton and subsidiaries included!
Contractors outside of military authority!
Confusing discipline and responsibility!

V-P Cheney was CEO of Haliburton!
Insiders 2001, this was uncertain!
Private contractors are "only for profit!"
This arrangement does not deserve credit!

PRE-EMPTION

Pre-emptive ideas of war are dubious!
Bush/Cheney Administration used this!
The Iraq War has become a real disaster!
Over 5000 Americans casualties suffered!

Innumerable Iraqis injured or dead!
  Numerous veterans became injured!
    Brain injuries, loss of limbs, PTSD!
      These problems are carried home!

By 2014, estimate $1.7 trillion expended!
  Cost of victims' care is not even included!
    Economists estimate $3 trillion overall
      What can justify this pre-emptive war?

Pre-emption is seen as not being attacked!
  But speculation pre-emptors might act!
    Pre-emptors take initiative before attack!
      What justifies preliminary war action?

MORE AMBIGUITY

Reagan, 1983, had Congressional approval
  But actual war in Lebanon did not occur
    His invasion of Grenada not acted upon!
      1991 attack on Iraq for occupying Kuwait!

No Congressional declaration in 1991
  To invade and occupy Afghanistan!
    In 2003, Bush/Cheney beyond Congress
      Invaded Iraq so two wars were pursued!

Political leaders can abuse authority!
  Unaware they can act unconsciously!
    Presidents, Royalties, Dictators
      May not recognize they are abusers!

America's three branches of government!
  Serving to balance power of their offices!

Examples of abuse are very numerous!
Pretending as civil servants is dubious!

Congress may control or neglect!
Legislative proposals as their acts!
Supreme Courts may act like God!
Presidents may wield power as a rod!

Governments may engage in war!
Identifying enemies to slaughter!
These aggressive actions can occur!
To overwhelm enemies as others!

WEALTH

Superiority deceives many wealthy
That they should dominate lowly!
Unequal power is exerted frequently!
By leading poor persons into slavery!

Control is assumed by the wealthy!
Tempting them to dominate cruelly!
Justice often favors the controllers
Stifling the lives of those poorer!

Money is abused by many as power!
Rather than a resource as sharers!
Passing on the wealth to inheritors
Perpetuates inequities to successors!

Assumption of power is contagious!
Frequently this is very unconscious!
This can result in serious injustice!
Social problems can become a mess!

PASSIVE USE of POWER

Ignoring problems becomes passive!
Not recognizing what are injustices!
When citizens do not become active
Persons may not know how to live!

Passive aggression is very slippery!
But adolescents learn this quickly!
Agree with the authority figures
Then do not comply as actors!

People who utilize nonviolence
Misunderstood as being passive!
But nonviolence can be very active!
Defeating those who are aggressive!

When controlled by aggression
Different tactics for one's actions!
Direct opposition is not warranted
While discipline is recommended!

APPROPRIATE USE of POWER

This topic is very challenging!
How not to become controlling!
Fighting back is not recommended
It results in more violence un-ended!

Violence results in more violence!
A vicious cycle has continuance!
How can humans live peacefully?
By living together respectfully!

Between aggression and passivity
　Is "ASSERTIVENESS as priority!
　　Asserting our own personal rights
　　　Without violating others' rights!

Assertiveness requires discipline
　Controlling one's own reactions
　　This undoes aggressive actions
　　　By not responding with aggression!

PRACTICES

Instead of accusing other persons
　Who often state: "you accusations!"
　　Reply with one's own responses
　　　"I..." rather than accusatory "You...."

Being in touch with oneself
　Helps self-control as ourselves!
　　Attacking aggressors is unworkable!
　　　This soon heightened confrontations!

Assertiveness stands for one's rights!
　Undoing the aggressor's own attacks!
　　After practice, these are effective
　　　Appropriate and also expressive!

Countering aggression is recommended
　Plus, passive-aggression as practiced!
　　Assertiveness needs personal discipline
　　　To become effective and also responsive!

C. CONNECTING with POLICY-MAKERS

This inter-disciplinary field
    Provides exceptional yield.
        It's approach to problem-solving
            Leads to ethical change-making.

        First, you define the problem;
      This is essential to deal with them.
  Poor definition is also troublesome;
Other procedures are cumbersome.

Then comes a search for solutions;
    By avoiding just pet resolutions.
        Complexity may be necessary
           To be locally and globally.

        Solutions need to be ethical,
      And also be cross-cultural!
  It is essential to be thorough
So wide coverage is possible.

DISCOVERING HUMANKIND

From the Viet Nam War to peace
    A rough journey with little ease!
        Too many persons under stress;
           Our lesson is not to regress!

        Many children and women lost;
      Soldiers and civilians suffered costs!
  As human beings suffered very badly
And veterans experienced traumatically!

When will global leaders learn?
How many civilizations have to burn?
Why do not wars lead to learning?
Will humans ever avoid suffering?

Can we rediscover bridge-building?
The best designs are for connecting!
Bringing separated people together!
Finding mutuality is so much better!

Cultivating our best human qualities!
Discovering neighbors peaceably!
Encouraging healthy livelihoods!
Building our joint neighborhoods.

Addressing challenges together;
Helping to be problem-solvers.
Nourishing our best humanity!
By living together beneficially!

PURSING GOALS

Humanity has major challenges;
Finding peace, security and justice!
Leaders and citizens collaborating1
So that we have hopeful living!

Goals are for safe environments;
Protection by civil governments!
Food and water for health living;
So, children can grow up thriving!

By addressing problems together
As people become collaborators!

Goals of good health and education
Plus, respect for global religions.

Collaborative teamwork is needed;
Science and technology pursued!
Environmental health achieved
Global warming also relieved!

This requires intentional living;
Humankind giving and receiving!
Positive goals worth achieving
As humanity's future is unfolding!

COLLABORATING INTERNATIONALLY

We can collaborate internationally;
This adds to experiences globally.
Our world expands cross-culturally;
For fostering peace for us as timely.

n 1995, I have a conference in Nepal;
Carol and I traveled then to India.
Together, we toured TAJ MAHAL
This structure is impressive for all.

Organizational Development conferred;
I presented a professional program.
Warsaw University invited me
But teaching responsibilities.

In, 1997, Thomas John invited me
To both teach and consult in India.
My daughter, Susan, developed cancer;
Later that year, she then did recover!

At Union Christian College, I taught;
  Part of Mahatma Gandhi University.
    Developing a Masters Degree in Psychology;
      This bolstered their department's credibility.

      In 2001, an invitation to Manipal University;
    To fill their Endowed Chair for Peace.
  Then 9/11 attack on New York City;
Restored my injured e-mail "MIT."

Carol bravely traveled again to India!
  Demonstrating that she had courage!
    We safely returned after teaching;
      Part of our International traveling.

- STAYING CONNECTED!![27]

Yes, we are all inter-connected
  This is also how we are protected!
    We are held together in a bond;
      Both here on Earth and beyond.

      We have important relationships;
    Human and sub-human connecting.
  All living creatures are significant
As connections are important.

We have reasons then to celebrate;
  By recognizing how we create!
    Creativity is our special gift;
      Giving all of us an uplift!

---

[27] AARP's Social Network.

Connecting in several ways:
Connected, we can engage!
We can then be equipped,
Jointly, we can educate!!!

Can we connect responsibly?
Yes, we can accountability.
Bouncing back with resiliency
Expressing joy with intensity.

We function best together;
The willing can be stronger!
Jointly, we can be supportive
Jointly, we will be connective!

Is Putin acting as an old devil?
His own warring is now evil!
Ukraine receives heavy bombing;
Putin's decisions are terrifying!

Ukrainians are fleeing for cover;
Hoping the fighting will be over.
Different parties are polarized;
Neither side know wat is wise.

Is Putin wanting more control?
Does he hope Ukrainians will go?
Is he trying to be and Emperor?
Does he want them to expire?

His actions provoke questions;
Will he engage in transactions?
He is causing many uncertainties;
He is also creating many enemies.

Putin is staring more hostilities;
   Can the Russians be more friendly?
      People are facing many uncertainties;
         What will become of their destiny?

      Europe has had an unusual history!
     Will leaders address these mysteries?
   They are facing many new challenges;
No need now to seek more revenge.

Is Putin acting as an old devil?
   His own warring is now evil!
      Ukraine receives heavy bombing;
         Putin's decisions are terrifying!

      Ukrainians are fleeing for cover;
     Hoping the fighting will be over.
   Different parties are polarized;
Neither side know wat is wise.

Is Putin wanting more control?
   Does he hope Ukrainians will go?
      Is he trying to be and Emperor?
         Does he want them to expire?

      His actions provoke questions;
     Will he engage in transactions?
   He is causing many uncertainties;
He is also creating many enemies.

Putin is starting more hostilities;
   Can the Russians be more friendly?
      People are facing many uncertainties;
         What will become of their destiny?

Europe has had an unusual history!
Will leaders address these mysteries?
They are facing many new challenges;
No need now to seek more revenge.

Putin's invasion of the nation of Ukraine
Does contaminate trust to now remain.
He is corrupting humanity with strain;
International relations now refrain!

DIS-CONNECTING

Opposite concepts do occur;
Their outcomes ae not sure.
These occasions catch attention
Disconnecting has apprehension.

Marriages can end by divorce;
Tensions are present, of course.
Legal separation then occurs,
Such disconnection closes doors.

Children are then directly affected;
Disaffection of parents has occurred.
The couples' bond of love is broken
Unkind words are often spoken.

Terminating marriage has consequences;
Perhaps some relief in many instances.
Any angry emotions maybe severed;
Once lovers! But now separated.

Divorce results in termination;
Of marital status; not parenthood.

Children have their own loyalties
They try, but have discontinuities.

Separation has its limitations,
Human beings avoid separation.
We often want to be together
By joining, we live better.

Persons thrive by connecting;
Together is our way of working.
Jointly may result in thriving;
This results many are hoping.

AGGRESSIVE USE of POWER

Unconscious use & abuse or power
Contrasting with conscious users!
Often aggression can be spontaneous
Used without balancing impulsiveness!

Power by humans is ambiguous!
Used unconsciously & conscious!
Power may be open or disguised!
Often power is used by surprise!

Authority figures express power!
Parents control those younger!
Teachers use class discipline!
Police control criminal & victim!

Adults may be abusive to children!
Spouses may control their mates!
Police can arrest the suspicious!
Robbers may become malicious!

RECOGNIZING AGGRESSION

Bullying can be done openly
  Picking victims quite instantly!
    Some victims prompt bullying!
      Bully-victim make a "Pairing!"

Bosses have major responsibilities!
  Then subordinates become utilities!
    Government leaders have authority!
      Governing people in their citizenry!

Assumptions see power consciously!
  Abuses may be done unconsciously!
    Neither party may have awareness!
      Until abuses become obvious messes!

Professionals may overwhelm clients!
  Physicians may over-control patients!
    Clergy may serve as if they are God!
      Judges may make their rulings weird!

WHAT ARE ABUSES of POWER?

Is capital punishment abusive?
  Debate now continues as useful!
    What is bases for death sentences?
      Can humans decide without biases?

Do humans have rights for guns?
  Is it provided in 2nd amendment?
    To bear arms as a personal right?
      Only intended for national defense?

How can Presidents legally initiate war?
Or does Congress serve as the "Decider?"
After WW II, has this been abused?
Consider how this power is used!

Korean War had no Congressional approval!
Over 50,000 American casualties resulted!
Plus, Vietnam was the "American War!"
Bay of Tonkin Resolutions undeclared!

Are these abuses or are they neglect?
Is Combat against ISIS ever correct?
Obama seeks Congressional approval!
To declare war limited to three years!

Ambiguity continues for starting wars!
When invasions do occur, it is clearer!
Attacks by any terrorists is a puzzle!
No nation is considered as terrorists!

WHAT IS OUR DUTY?

Soldiers report to duty in uniform!
U.S. is defended by men and women!
Soldiers will obey as their orders!
Defending U.S. interests or borders!

Volunteers have not been enough!
Without a draft, this is very tough!
So "private contractors" do bidding!
Private authority, not military drilling!

But contracting has become abusive!
Haliburton and subsidiaries included!

Contractors outside of military authority!
Confusing discipline and responsibility!

V-P Cheney was CEO of Haliburton!
Insiders 2001, this was uncertain!
Private contractors are "only for profit!"
This arrangement does not deserve credit!

PRE-EMPTION

Pre-emptive ideas of war are dubious!
Bush/Cheney Administration used this!
The Iraq War has become a real disaster!
Over 5000 Americans casualties suffered!

Innumerable Iraqis injured or dead!
Numerous veterans became injured!
Brain injuries, loss of limbs, PTSD!
These problems are carried home!

By 2014, estimate $1.7 trillion expended!
Cost of victims' care is not even included!
Economists estimate $3 trillion overall
What can justify this pre-emptive war?

Pre-emption is seen as not being attacked!
But speculation pre-emptors might act!
Pre-emptors take initiative before attack!
What justifies preliminary war action?

MORE AMBIGUITY

Reagan, 1983, had Congressional approval
But actual war in Lebanon did not occur
His invasion of Grenada not acted upon!
1991 attack on Iraq for occupying Kuwait!

No Congressional declaration in 1991
To invade and occupy Afghanistan!
In 2003, Bush/Cheney beyond Congress
Invaded Iraq so two wars were pursued!

Political leaders can abuse authority!
Unaware they can act unconsciously!
Presidents, Royalties, Dictators
May not recognize they are abusers!

America's three branches of government!
Serving to balance power of their offices!
Examples of abuse are very numerous!
Pretending as civil servants is dubious!

Congress may control or neglect!
Legislative proposals as their acts!
Supreme Courts may act like God!
Presidents may wield power as a rod!

Governments may engage in war!
Identifying enemies to slaughter!
These aggressive actions can occur!
To overwhelm enemies as others!

WEALTH

Superiority deceives many wealthy
That they should dominate lowly!
Unequal power is exerted frequently!
By leading poor persons into slavery!

Control is assumed by the wealthy!
Tempting them to dominate cruelly!
Justice often favors the controllers
Stifling the lives of those poorer!

Money is abused by many as power!
Rather than a resource as sharers!
Passing on the wealth to inheritors
Perpetuates inequities to successors!

Assumption of power is contagious!
Frequently this is very unconscious!
This can result in serious injustice!
Social problems can become a mess!

PASSIVE USE of POWER

Ignoring problems becomes passive!
Not recognizing what are injustices!
When citizens do not become active
Persons may not know how to live!

Passive aggression is very slippery!
But adolescents learn this quickly!
Agree with the authority figures
Then do not comply as actors!

People who utilize nonviolence
  Misunderstood as being passive!
    But nonviolence can be very active!
      Defeating those who are aggressive!

When controlled by aggression
  Different tactics for one's actions!
    Direct opposition is not warranted
      While discipline is recommended!

APPROPRIATE USE of POWER

This topic is very challenging!
  How not to become controlling!
    Fighting back is not recommended
      It results in more violence un-ended!

Violence results in more violence!
  A vicious cycle has continuance!
    How can humans live peacefully?
      By living together respectfully!

Between aggression and passivity
  Is "ASSERTIVENESS as priority!
    Asserting our own personal rights
      Without violating others' rights!

Assertiveness requires discipline
  Controlling one's own reactions
    This undoes aggressive actions
      By not responding with aggression!

PRACTICES

Instead of accusing other persons
Who often state: "you" accusations!
Reply with one's own responses
"I..." rather than accusatory "You...."

Being in touch with oneself
Helps self-control as ourselves!
Attacking aggressors is unworkable!
This soon heightened confrontations!

Assertiveness stands for one's rights!
Undoing the aggressor's own attacks!
After practice, these are effective
Appropriate and also expressive!

Countering aggression is recommended
Plus, passive-aggression as practiced!
Assertiveness needs personal discipline
To become effective and also responsive!

DISCOVERING HUMANKIND

From the Viet Nam War to peace
A rough journey with little ease!
Too many persons under stress;
Our lesson is not to regress!

Many children and women lost;
Soldiers and civilians suffered costs!
As human beings suffered very badly
And veterans experienced traumatically!

When will global leaders learn?
How many civilizations have to burn?
Why do not wars lead to learning?
Will humans ever avoid suffering?

Can we rediscover bridge-building?
The best designs are for connecting!
Bringing separated people together!
Finding mutuality is so much better!

Cultivating our best human qualities!
Discovering neighbors peaceably!
Encouraging healthy livelihoods!
Building our joint neighborhoods.

Addressing challenges together;
Helping to be problem-solvers.
Nourishing our best humanity!
By living together beneficially!

PURSING GOALS

Humanity has major challenges;
Finding peace, security and justice!
Leaders and citizens collaborating1
So that we have hopeful living!

Goals are for safe environments;
Protection by civil governments!
Food and water for health living;
So, children can grow up thriving!

By addressing problems together
As people become collaborators!

Goals of good health and education
Plus, respect for global religions.

Collaborative teamwork is needed;
Science and technology pursued!
Environmental health achieved
Global warming also relieved!

This requires intentional living;
Humankind giving and receiving!
Positive goals worth achieving
As humanity's future is unfolding!
Part of our International traveling.

MORE CONNECTIONS NEEDED!

More bridges are needed into the future!
Connecting Africans, Australians and Europe!
You are now encouraged to now participate;
Because global connections cannot wait!

Euro-Asians have been connected a long time;
Now more railroads travel this new silk route!
Technology already has the world connected!
Sea and air travel will handle part of this load!

New ideas emerge from making these connections!
"One Belt; One Road!" OBOR[28] is an abbreviation!
Key challenges will need more global solutions!
Such as global warming and vast pollutions!

---

[28] Herve', Juvin, 2019, "The Geopolitics of the New Silk Road," <u>American Affairs</u>, Vol. III, Number 1.

You are invited to undertake new approaches!
Humanity now needs to give attention for futures!
Teamwork helps to address these global difficulties!
Posterity will benefit from your own team involvements!

HEATING the EARTH [29]

I recently finished reading:
    How to Avoid a Climate Disaster.[30]
        We are challenged with warming;
            Our generations are contributing.

        We are called to be stewards, [31]
    This is our duty as Christians.
Our vehicles consume oil
Carbon Dioxide as resultant.

We all have responsibilities;
    So let us utilize our abilities.
        Future generations count on us;
            So let us all honor their trust!

        Each one of us have a conscience;
    We can implement global science.
Delaying will become complicated;
It is time for us to act---not to wait!

---

[29] Middents, G., Heating the Earth: Global Warming, iUniverse Books.

[30] Gates, Bill, 2021, How to Avoid a Climate Disaster, Random House.

[31] Bible: Old Testament, Genesis 2.

MEANINGFUL CONNECTIONS: [32]

Connecting enriches our human living;
   This is also how we discover meaning!
      Our attachments help our relations;
         We become involved in giving and taking.

         Interacting expands our perspective;
     These relationships become interactive.
   Relationships are the bases for connecting
Such mutuality enriches our own meaning!

We do have numerous connections:
   These help all of global civilizations.
      Many have telephones to connect;
         These connections are very direct.

We also have some vast highways,
   Continents connected by waterways;
      Airplanes have many flying routes;
         Around the world by ship routes.

         Railroads cross over continents;
   These all to multi-thousands.
With many stops along the way;
Connections are here to stay!

Asia and Europe are connected;
   East and West coasts of U.S.A.
      Africa is connected by ships,
         Passengers can make long trips!

---

[32] Brown, Brene, "Meaningful Connections" Atlas of the Heart.

STAYING CONNECTED!! [33]

Yes, we are now all inter-connected
This is also how we are protected!
We are held together in a bond;
Both here on Earth and beyond.

We have important relationships;
Human and sub-human connecting.
All living creatures are significant
As connections are important.

We have reasons then to celebrate;
By recognizing how we create!
Creativity is our special gift;
Giving all of us an uplift!

Connecting in several ways:
Connected, we can engage!
We can then be equipped,
Jointly, we can educate!!!

Can we connect responsibly?
Yes, we can accountability.
Bouncing back with resiliency
Expressing joy with intensity.

We function best together;
The willing can be stronger!
Jointly, we can be supportive
Jointly, we will be a collective!

---

[33] AARP's Social Network.

Bibliography

Armstrong, K., *The Case for God,*

Czitsentmyhali, M., *FLOW,*

Difucio., D., 4/1/22, "Dating Bhemoth sees more human interactions…" *Dallas Morning News.*

Doggett, J.N., September 1, 2021, "Classrooms are where magic happens, *Dallas Morning News.*

Frankl, Viktor, 1963 *Man's Search for Meaning*

ibid., Sources of Meaning

Gallery, Joyce, *Gallery of Hope Stones*

Grant, R. and Cobbert, A., "New Chapter," Smithsonian, Dec. 2021

Hedges, C., *War is the Power that Give Men Meaning.*

Job, the book in the *Bible: The Old Testament*

Jung, C., *Collected Work of Carl Jung.*

Laubach, F., *Adult Ways for Reading.*

McGrath, A., 2013, *Surprised by Meaning: Science, Faith and How We make Senso of Things, Westminster John Knox Press,*

Melugin, R., Personal communication.

Middents, G., 1989, *The Gift of Life: Giving and Receiving, MSS.*

ibid., BRIDGING FEAR AND PEACE: From Bullying to Doing Justice.

Nietzsche, F., _Collected Works._

Norris, Kathleen, _Embracing Life of Meaning._ Ramadan, T., 2012, _The Quest for Meaning._ Strand London, Penquin Books.

Tillich, P., _The Ground of Being_

Zaretsky, R., 2013 _A Life Worth Living: Albert Camus and the Quest for Meaning._ Harvard University Press.

Printed in the United States
by Baker & Taylor Publisher Services